WRITING THE GOLDEN STATE

WRITING THE GOLDEN STATE: THE NEW LITERARY TERRAIN OF CALIFORNIA

EDITED BY

CARRIBEAN FRAGOZA
ROMEO GUZMÁN
SAMINE JOUDAT

FOREWORD BY SUSAN STRAIGHT | ILLUSTRATIONS BY FERNANDO MENDEZ CORONA

ANGEL CITY PRESS
LOS ANGELES PUBLIC LIBRARY

CONTENTS

FOREWORD

SUSAN STRAIGHT

California, Califas, Cali, Calafia—all names for the Golden State where I was born and the names I've heard throughout my decades of living here, the names written on my junior high walls, the legends and songs and whispers and family stories of our communities in Riverside and San Bernardino counties, from the Lorenzo Trujillo family who arrived in 1843 and whose descendants I see all the time, to my in-laws who arrived from Mississippi and Oklahoma in the 1920s and 1950s, to my own mother who became a citizen in 1963, to the new neighbors on my street who arrived from Michoacan, Mexico only a few years ago.

Everyone knows the names of the iconic writers who are said to represent this vast state, the essays and stories we've been handed hundreds of times by outsiders to tell us about our own places. In *Writing the Golden State*, Carribean Fragoza, Romeo Guzmán, and Samine Joudat offer readers new and established voices to tell fresh stories about California, stories to bring readers to places they need to go. Their "Postcards" series, published in *Boom California*, functions like the best found postcards purchased at a thrift store or yard sale or picked up on a sidewalk. Vivid rectangles with an image that might be mysterious, with surprises deep inside the landscape, with the edges of legends to be found.

The collection travels from the Mexico border, where the Golden State truly begins, to the Coachella Valley, the Antelope Valley, San Diego and Orange Counties, to the San Joaquin Valley and the vast reaches of the Central Valley. In Riverside County, there are Duroville and Corona. And in Los Angeles County, a myriad of stories from the LA that outsiders might never have seen.

The exuberance and tenderness of Marco Vera's love letter to his *abuelo*'s *fruteria* begins with hilarity and joy—Vera was raised two blocks from the border between Mexico and California, and his essay is a beautiful opening.

Ruxandra Guidi takes a journey to one of my most beloved places in the world, the Coachella Valley, not the "Coachella" strangers know, but the community of Duroville, where farmworkers battle to create a home.

Wendy Cheng's wry portrait of Rancho Santa Fe, one of the most wealthy places in the state, takes us to the lush garden cultivated by her parents and grandparents to grow a home where home was uneasy.

Ruth Nolan's vivid essay of fire's aftermath in the Mojave National Preserve, a place driven through, thought of as barren, gives it life: "A red-tailed hawk circles above, riding on a fit of ash-strewn wind that is spinning into a dark dust devil."

Kenji Liu writes of the fig, most treasured fruit growing wild or cultured in every garden or field in California. Melissa Mora Hidalgo's piece describes the legacy of her family, their discovery of an indigenous ancestor whose epic life encompassed San Luis Obispo, East Los Angeles, and decades of California history not often seen.

Heading north, George Sanchez-Tello sings a punk rock version of Salinas, while Brynn Saito writes a beautiful elegy and chorus to her family's San Joaquin Valley that belongs with the best writing of that place: Fresno, Reedley, and Dinuba, where her mother's oldest brother was killed. "He died on Raisin Day," she says, "Dinuba's annual harvest festival, September of 1976."

And in Los Angeles County, and the City of Angels, writers give us places few have known well. Jenise Miller takes readers on a mouthwatering tour of the Black Panamanian communities where far-flung families gather for memory and feast. Carolyn Dunn's wistful portrait of her mother's life in Watts and San Pedro, and her own caretaking of that mother, is lovely. David Ulin walks Los Angeles, and sees secrets.

This collection finds new breezes and winds flowing through the mountains, valleys, cities, and suburbs, through the deserts high and low, through the sidewalks, parks, parties, and streets, the cemeteries and fields and rivers of our state—so many new and established voices, so many wonderful tales.

INTRODUCTION

CARRIBEAN FRAGOZA, ROMEO GUZMÁN, SAMINE JOUDAT

Legg Lake in the Whittier Narrows is a place of return. Generations of families flock here to celebrate birthdays, exercise, barbecue, and fish along its banks. It's a place to salute a sunset at the side of a friendly octopus, as its last rays recede behind the western rim of the valley. Concrete monsters are worn smooth by the bodies of countless children, climbing and sliding down their colorful limbs and tails. They always face the water, and we all learn to face it, too.

A place to be held, embraced by hills and the San Gabriel Mountains, cupped in the intimacy of the narrows. The river is a portal between worlds.

Like a fire is for gathering, so is this body of water, both for solitude or for intimate company.

It retains the ancient memory of the land, of this place that has been home to ancestors for more years than we know how to count. Where urbanization has cemented over, or channeled into regulated water systems, or erased so many streams and brooks from the land altogether, some bodies of water have persisted, by their own volition as well as the efforts of people who worked to conserve them. Certainly, Legg Lake and the Whittier Narrows are constructed spaces, curated as parks that offer the public access to essential green space and recreation. Picnic areas, sports facilities, bike paths, and exercise equipment serve as essential health and wellness resources for all communities, especially working-class families in the San Gabriel Valley.

But beyond and before infrastructure, more than water pumps that keep the lake from becoming stagnant, or sprinklers that keep park lawns green, is something deeper that nourishes the land and continues to call us.

Water as subterranean
Water as embedded memory
Water as language of its own
Water as a call of return

It calls birds: a regular stop on their migratory paths.

It calls babies: watch them run to it immediately, ready to splash onto its algae-laden shore. Watch how they are eventually lulled to sleep by it.

For many of us, the lake holds our spirit for safekeeping. When we are lost, we know where to find ourselves. We return and cast a blurred gaze over its sparking waters, to rest, to allow our hearts to speak without the work of words.

As one of the largest green spaces in Southern California, Whittier Narrows is singular. And, yet, like many spaces throughout California, it contains multiple layers of history and multiple uses. There is cement at the bottom of the lake, but the attachment to place, the memories, are very real, even if often overlooked in larger histories of Southern California. For the last decade, we—Romeo Guzmán and Carribean Fragoza—have diligently worked with community members, scholars, and artists to document, write, and creatively experience the history of two cities just north of Whittier Narrows: South El Monte and El Monte. With *East of East: The Making of Greater El Monte*, we aspired to combine academic rigor with the beauty and intimacy of long-form journalism and to place these two cities on the map. We launched the creative nonfiction series titled "Postcards" in *Boom California* to center marginalized voices and forgotten, overlooked, poorly understood, and deeply loved cities, places, and regions throughout California. After publishing a dozen essays online, together with Samine Joudat, we accepted an additional twelve and published them all in the book you now hold.

Writing the Golden State creates a new cartography of California through literature and language that is as much about marking and representing space, as it is about storytelling. Collectively, the essays challenge the dominant historical narratives about California neighborhoods that reinscribe xenophobic, ableist, racist, classist, and patriarchal attitudes. Like all edited projects, this one is a product of its editors and an open call. It has gaps and omissions, but nonetheless contributes to our collective knowledge about California. Instead of measuring or forecasting the relative health of the "California Dream," the authors provide an on-the-ground and honest portrait of the state's past and present. There are no promises, lofty projections, or an ingenious panacea that will wash away the state's sins.

Writing in search of what Brynn Saito calls the *genius loci*—the spirit of a place—*Writing the Golden State* pries into the themes of familial lineage, migration and displacement, land and housing, youth culture and work, and national belonging and identity, stretching back in some cases to the beginning of the twentieth century, and in others to the early postwar years. The twenty-four essays represent a wide geography of California, from urban centers and the coast to smaller towns and the desert. Lesser-known areas of the Central Valley like Dinuba are featured. Moving south, the sprawl of Los Angeles is covered in various multitudes, while San Diego and Mexicali, on the edge of the US–Mexico border, round out the project's geographical coverage. The heart and strength of these stories lie in the rich vantages of their authors. The cohort includes queer, Chicanx, Indigenous, Black Panamanian, African American, and Asian American writers, including emerging writers like Jenise Miller and established authors including Wendy Cheng, Myriam Gurba, David L. Ulin, and Ruth Nolan.

Authors hail from a range of disciplines that include literature, poetry, filmmaking, journalism, podcasting, cultural criticism, American studies, and urban planning.

As the world tries to emerge from COVID and place it in the past tense, the challenges that face California and the nation remain ever-present. As uncontrolled fire becomes as common as the Santa Ana winds, writer and former firefighter Ruth Nolan guides us through the Mojave desert:

> Every desert fire, past and present, especially ones I worked on and even now, feels deeply personal to me. As I watched media coverage of the Dome Fire play out online, I reacted as I usually do during every major desert fire event over the years. I was frustrated and felt displaced to not be there in person, doing something to help with fire suppression operations—shovel work cutting fire line, perhaps, or helping at the makeshift helicopter operations base.

Jenise Miller, Cassandra Lane, and David Helps examine housing, gentrification, and displacement in Los Angeles, while Sue Mark and Heidi Herrera write about North Oakland. Following her father, Jennifer Carr takes us to San Pedro and the influx of automation:

> As for now—we don't know what's going to happen. Maersk uses microchips in the containers and even on the docks, plugged into robots to do the work my father spent hours of his week planning out. He'd come home, dusted yellow with spray chalk from marking steel slabs and coils, marking the yard for placing the steel slabs, coils, and plywood to be loaded onto trucks or railcars, double-checking bills of lading, somehow sorting cargo the way a conductor guides a symphony or the Sorcerer Supreme bends the world at his will.

The suburbs, a perennial topic for students of California, emerge in a few essays, including Wendy Cheng's "In Rancho Santa Fe," Elaine Lewinnek's "Park Place Material," and Myriam Gurba's "El Corrido del Copete." Rather than the idealistic tranquility portrayed in popular culture such as the 1990s sitcom *The Wonder Years*, or the sensationalized suburban mom-turned-drug dealer in *Weeds*, our authors cover the 'burbs with both historical depth and intimacy. Cheng narrates the development of a wealthy suburb in north county San Diego that was built to embody and represent the Spanish fantasy past for white Americans: "In 1986, when I was nine and my brother was ten, my parents moved us to a place I have never claimed, a place that has never claimed me." Lewinnek traces the rise of homeowners associations and the privatization of public space, including a dog park. In Santa Maria Valley, Gurba revisits an epic junior high school battle between a white girl named Karen and a Chicana named Jenni and places it in the larger history of American conquest: "Gringos had been pushing Mexicans to the edge since they first trudged into California. Desperation turned us into desperados, and after they laid claim to our land, money, and bodies, they left us a single valuable to defend: our reputations."

Taken as a whole, *Writing The Golden State* leaves an indelible imprint of a California not often portrayed on the Hollywood screen, the state newspapers' front pages, or the school curriculum. Here, the reader finds in the words of these authors and the illustrations by Fernando Corona, a taste of California that is deviant and recalcitrant, proud and humble, joyful and communal. It is a California that reclaims the beauty of the unwanted, the quotidian, and the out-of-place. It is the story of the neighborhood fruit stand that belonged to a beloved grandfather, the memories of family and home, fig trees, war, pogroms, punk shows, block parties, and immigrants refusing to conform to lesser-than subjectivities. Here, you'll find voices dedicated to, in the words of D.J. Waldie, "becoming the Californians that California needs." Like the birds and babies drawn to Whittier Narrows, our authors gravitate to place in hopes of unraveling its layers and potentially creating new routes to the future.

MEMORIES OF MY TATA'S *FRUTERÍA*

MARCO VERA

We never ate salads. World-class mechanics drive lemons; world-class musicians pawn instruments. Know-it-all scholars would come to our store because the university was close by. All the math was done on a Scribe notebook, quietly, as a swamp cooler rocked you to sleep. Tripping out, because there is no other way to spend time in a fruit stand after morning setup duties. Art was there, always, always, always. In the way you stacked tomatoes. In the rotation of the avocados. In the Dutch angle tamarind candy. In the handcrafted, misspelled signage with the price collaged on neon bright fluorescent-colored paper.

There's a science and technique to opening *costales*. Just like there is to cleaning and bagging *cacahuates*. Or stacking bags of *carbon*. In the Malverde merchandise room, chaos was art, as Jesús's bust would watch over you trying to make sense of the merchandise rearrangement. A framed print of San Martin Caballero hung in the lobby open to the public where we played the nice *señora* ballads. Malverde was in the back, where the radios blared to a different beat, Punk and *Norteño* music. If you were a wiseass, you'd oversleep to stay in the air conditioning in the house next door where my grandparents lived. But the smell of garlic was too alluring. The *chile pico de pájaro* halo that adorned our day-to-day is something I miss every day. Many years later, the smells of dried *chile california* and *chile pasilla* still jump-start those memories.

I did some of my growing up in a fruit stand in Mexicali. Frutería Alejandrina. An establishment full of disaster, poor judgment, and reflections of a teenage memory. The funniest, most beautiful place to roll out the red carpet on being a peacock. *Toda la pinche vida carposa.*

My grandparents had a fruit stand on the northern border of a super, super nice part of town. Where governors lived, and the houses looked like marble mansions. Safe as houses even if that 'hood had a big ole graveyard, with gangs like "*Los Panteons*" referencing it. *Colonia Libertad*, the freedom neighborhood. A place where detached, lived-in people from the 'hood or posh intellectual fucks on their mistress dates would come by and purchase the bare essentials. It wasn't as tough as my neighborhood, which was two blocks away from the physical US–Mexico border, but it was poor, neighboring the richest part of town. Everything seemed more ironic. And those memories are crisper, because you don't have fear or crime clouding your overall existence and sadness. There were cute girls coming into the shop. Rocker girls. With money. The cruising strip was not too far away, in the rich part of town. My barrio was Amber Alert. My grandpa's barrio was divine. We were a border *frutería* in a border city, an assertion that you needed us; it was love amidst class war.

And once every week or so, Frutería Alejandrina had to restock. So we would drive back near my 'hood to downtown Mexicali, to a place full of wonder and smells and culture and a taste of all of México nicknamed "*La Yarda*." A double entendre poem in motion. Mercado Braulio Maldonado is known to all the locals as *La Yarda*. A place frozen in time. Founded by working people to be passed down to their offspring for generations to come. It was hot. It was absurd. It was full of lament and fast-paced driving decisions. It was millimetric. It was colorful. It was full of smiles and laughter. And sun. You had a stake in it. The United States was not far off. But the tale was everybody's. We had possession; we were awake. It was always day in *La Yarda*. If you saw it by night, you were a bit of a tourist.

Named after what was by all accounts a brutal and repressive governor, Mercado Braulio Maldonado is referred to as "*La Yarda*" for reasons unbeknownst to many. Local unofficial historians even claim it's a *pochismo*, a bastardization of the language, as the border always does, signifying "The Yard," due to all the loading docks filled with truckloads of fruit and vegetables lining the immense real estate. *La Yarda*, like any beautifully chaotic memory, is fiercely contested geographically. "Where does it start?" "Who started it where?" "Were you so-and-so neighbors back in 1962?"

But this is a postcard. A postcard to my grandfather, *a mi Tata*. Reverse psychology souls. We were both heavy breathing alcohol. Drinking ourselves away like little devils in a graveyard.

The kiosk where the mariachis and *taka takas* would wait for gigs was our parking departure. My cousin and my uncle would reiterate that I wasn't shit as they blew up their grandeur driving the van or crowded pickup truck, even when I didn't want their *Yarda* canonization or holiness. My grandma hated all of it, the restock. There was no love in that affair for her, unfortunately. Just separation. But I found peace there. Peace from social classes, genres of youth roleplay, it was all mixed up together. Beautifully. Low blows and all. An oasis for the shrink-wrapped battalions of drunks and nihilists dreaming of luxurious starlets at the magazine stand. The audience at the cockfight dishing out fables, day drinking. Euphoria.

My grandfather's journey as a merchant began in Culiacan, Sinaloa. His father married and remarried but always took his first-born son along with him, teaching him the trade, being the owner of a wholesale distributor that supplied its clients with fruits and vegetables from all over Mexico. Once he was of age, my grandfather's dad set him up with a fruit stand in Culiacan's Mercado Garmendia, where he met my grandmother, a client who would come in and ask the price of items individually, to see how much her handful of coins could afford her. My grandmother had been left behind by her widowed mother who migrated to the border town of Mexicali and formed a new family of her own in the border city. After her grandma passed away, my grandma was left to the care of an abusive aunt who would take a big bulk of her profits doing home-to-home manicures and pedicures. Out of desperation, she asked my grandfather if she could live with him; he in turn left his girlfriend, and they moved in together with consent from both families, later starting a family of their own.

Years later, my grandmother's mother came back to Culiacan from Mexicali on a trip to reconnect with her daughter and her family, and that established constant travel between both cities. My mother was taken to Mexicali at the age of five to practically be raised by her aunt and grandma, but when they wanted to adopt her at the age of thirteen, my grandmother refused, and back to Sinaloa she went. My mom would eventually move to Mexicali as a young adult, having grown tired of not being allowed to study or work where she wanted. Taking advantage of a vacation to the border city, she found independence and did not return. Some of her sisters and her brother would follow the promise of borderland employment. My grandmother would later follow her children and her mother to the border city, reuniting three different generations of family affected by distance. My grandfather, now nearly alone in Culiacan with very little money and no business connections after a series of poor decisions, moved to Mexicali to rejoin his family.

My grandfather would have a humble reinvention in Mexicali as a *birria* taco vendor with a cart outside the city's railroad station, as passenger trains arrived and departed. One day, he caught the eye of a couple of young men who were kids when he owned fruit stands in Culiacan, guys that couldn't believe he didn't own his own business as he did back in their home state. They offered to give him a loan to start up a new business in Mexicali, supplying him with all the merchandise needed to commence what my grandfather would graciously call Frutería Alejandrina, in honor of the young men's business of the same name. Years later, with no more credit to pay and the property ownership under his belt, my grandfather had built what we all considered our home away from home, that beloved *frutería* forever etched in our memory.

There'd be rich people who would roll into Frutería Alejandrina, asking what it took to make a yummy guacamole. They would all have that same face of discovery. *La Yarda* was no different. It even had a local bus station by the mariachi kiosk that picked people up and dropped them off, one farm at a time, to restock, next to world-class vehicles and air-conditioned wine and cheese connoisseurs. But it was also a party. A playing field in a police state for migrants. Where self-made people unmount toward commerce. Where you could build a party from scratch, get different styles and sizes of piñatas, the ultimate Mexican *dulces*, theme-party candy bags... It was a place where you could see humans connected with nature, disconnect from it and package it. Signmaker commissions highlighted storefronts, restaurants, worker

bars and gay bars, barbershops, *banda* music for hire, bass drums, and mariachi and *Norteño* groups' vans.

Nowadays, it's a fascist state battle between wannabe gentrifiers "rehabilitating downtown," police harassing immigrants, divide-and-conquer Christians, and no end to justify the means. It's a place of constant relocation anyway. The tacos from El Jefe were better when he was down in the pit and outdoors, not his brick-and-mortar three blocks up, years later. Food at a marketplace tastes better when eaten standing up. These are facts.

If one business was struggling, others could relieve it. There was store-to-store credit. Grin and bear it was *La Yarda*'s mission statement. If you were young and thought you were enlightened, nobody cared. You still had to arrange the wooden crates along the wall. My cousin and I would wake up at night to drink; that was our dawn. Dawn was our afternoon—we would be so hungover. Everything was an interminable binge and a hangover. And on the street, there was always a scam, always a story. Men that cry to take your money. Professional actors. Cons. "Let me tell you something..." Weird caressing holds from grimy sausage fingers. All downtowns are beset by ghosts.

At Frutería Alejandrina, my grandfather and I could go days together working and hanging out without talking much, just reading *El Libro Vaquero* or watching classic movies from Mexico's Golden Age on the De Pelicula channel. When we'd visit *La Yarda*, we could both sense the status differences amidst businesses. The cold-storage room owners had personalized gold rings on several fingers; the daughters of the wholesalers wore designer jeans and ordered workers around. One could only imagine the lavish parties where they did the same. The rehab center fugitives wore rope around their waists, their hair flailing around looking for the "Ghostbusters van" to take them back to internment one last time. From the back of our van and in honor of all this chaos, we drank beers from the ice chest, between loading up, in between sugar wafer and Hot Cheeto bites, observing.

It was through this lens that my grandfather and I built our history together. We'd drink till all the perishables would become unsafe for consumption. If we were really hungover, we'd stop in at the *birrieria* and ask for coffee. I remember the first time I went; I said "Grandpa, I don't like coffee." "Shut up, just drink it. It's before ten." I'd get a coffee cup full of foamy, ice-cold beer prior to alcohol sale permits, then he'd order *birria* the right way. His background as a *birria* vendor informing his purchases, he only permitted us to go to this one *birria* spot. Where it was *birria de chivo*, none of that lamb or beef shit. With *machito* and *costilla*, *cebolla* y cilantro, *limones*, and salsa, all the different textures and flavors necessary to make it an experience. Then we'd get pretty faded ordering more *caguamas*, drinking them while sipping on our *consomé* with warm, handmade corn tortillas. I remember one time he ordered the *birria* head, and I ate the eye by mistake, but the meat would come off the warm tortilla scoop like butter.

After a *Yarda* restock, we'd get drunk with all the merchandise in the blazing heat, the chicken would thaw and go bad, and he'd invite his girlfriend over. We'd have to ask the restaurant owners to take away all the beer bottles, coffee and *consomé* cups, belonging to my cousin, my uncle, my grandpa, his lover, and her daughter—all having a dandy ol' time. We'd be greeted back at Alejandrina by a well-thumbed hose spray and disciplinary actions; one time I saw him get a whole bucket. It was sad but I would just escape to the cruising strip. And keep drinking. One time, my uncle and I got stoned and drunk while taking my grandpa to restock. Since it was the first restock of the year, my grandpa wanted to go to the downtown cathedral. He wouldn't go to church regularly, much less to confession, but he'd still cruise up and go get the host. Walked into a church full of police officers because it was their annual Mass; several of those cops knew us, especially my uncle. Never a bigger smile. Wasted. Watching my tipsy grandpa take communion, the only person not in blue. We left as soon as the host dissolved in his fiery breath.

When my grandpa would get very drunk, he'd start singing the lyrics to this one song: "Angelitos Negros." After claiming for years he wrote it, we discovered Javier Solis had sung it. So had Pedro Infante, famously. I only recently found out that Roberta Flack and Eartha Kitt did it, too.

> *Pintor si pintas con amor,*
> *Aunque la virgen sea blanca,*
> *Píntale angelitos negros*

It was grounding.

He would yell it! That feeling when he sang it. And I remember thinking, *I'll carry that underappreciated sentiment with me everywhere I'm headed.*

There is a court of appeals that succeeds when we remember our blurry selves; those intoxicating, enamored, simpler versions of ourselves. Like a greatest hits album. Not remembering the times we've been racist, idiotic, suicidal, sexist, apathetic, or truly, truly helplessly sad. Such are oral histories. There are landmarks that serve as living documents, testaments to when you and I were unstable and precarious. We've all driven past them after years of public transport to fall back in love with ourselves.

My tata's *frutería* was one of those chaotic commerce places that you could say was such without having to face your own mess at home.

There's one like it in your town.

IN RANCHO SANTA FE, WE WERE ORIENTALS

WENDY CHENG

In 1986, when I was nine and my brother was ten, my parents moved us to a place I have never claimed, a place that has never claimed me. Rancho Santa Fe, California: former land of the Santa Fe Railroad, whose twisted experiments created 100-foot tall stands of rare eucalyptus across the wealthy community. Lilian Rice's Spanish fantasy utopia. A golf course and a tennis club. The place I spent the better part of my youth, the place I first saw a ghost, the place my father died. The place where we were aliens, and alienated. And yet: it was home.

In Rancho Santa Fe, houses were full of pastels and light and tall arched entryways; they were pristine and cool as tombs. Dirt trails flanked the two-lane asphalt roads, and there were no sidewalks, mailboxes, or streetlights. The trails were made for people on horseback, an element in the landscape that might have made it feel rural, except that they led to the nearby, members-only golf course. Residents were proud of the rural fiction, though, and liked to refer to the town as "The Ranch."

In 1986, my mother and her business partners (a trio of Taiwanese immigrants) sold their first biotech company, and there was money to move up in the world. The house we bought was modest for the area: a four-bedroom ranch house built in the 1950s decorated with old linoleum, faded, pastel-striped wallpaper, and mustard-and-brown-colored tiles in the room that would be mine. The only thing I remember from when we went to look at the house is the earthy smell of ground beef frying in a pan, a smell that to me was exotic and slightly nauseating in its plainness—devoid of the sweet pungency of sizzling garlic, ginger, and soy sauce that infused most of the meat cooked in our house.

When our parents-to-be left Taiwan for graduate school in Detroit, Michigan and Madison, Wisconsin—taking the only pathway available to them out of an island under martial law—they severed their future children's connection to the land, to our relatives, to our ancestors, to culture, customs, and language. We were born, my brother and I, as stunted blank slates, both over- and under-determined by the racial and cultural identities we would never be able to fully grasp, while those were all most other people could see.

We lost the daily fish and vegetable and fruit market in Lotung, where my mother's mother went since she was a child in the 1930s, where everyone knew her, and the fishmonger knew exactly which fish she would want, where she could walk and speak with ease.

We lost the cracked land in Pingtung, where my father's father was an architect, and whose streets my father could traverse without a map even decades later, when he himself was an old man. (Watching him eat slices of sticky honeyed yams with a toothpick in the warm glow of the night market stalls at the age of sixty, I saw him become a child again.)

All my brother and I had was what we could see in front of us, every day: the graduate student family apartment at the University of Wisconsin with the red carpet and creaking metal swing set outside where we were each born and took our first steps. The small house with the brick fireplace in the Clairemont neighborhood of San Diego. The slightly larger house in Del Mar, where we became best friends with our neighbors' friendly freckled children, who ran barefoot with dirty feet. And then the ranch house on the big land in Rancho Santa Fe.

In Rancho Santa Fe, even though by then it was already 1986, we were Orientals. We were Orientals because there were so few of us at first: just ___ ___, in my brother's grade, whose family was so ridiculously rich they owned a pet monkey, and ___ ___, in my grade, whose father was white and wore a toupee. We were Orientals because my brother's big white athletic friends decided it would be fun to call him "Yang" (this was not our last name). We were Orientals because I was afraid to invite friends to eat dinner at our house, because they were grossed out and said so about things like squid ink on rice. We were Orientals because our parents never made friends with our friends' parents, not really, but only other Taiwanese people, who usually lived at least a half-hour drive away. We were Orientals because the local security patrol would slow down and tail my father when he was out walking by himself, and because my grandfather—who did not speak English and whose face was brown—was always assumed to be the gardener.

I didn't find out until much later that one of the reasons there were so few of "us" was because up until the 1970s, people of color were prohibited from living in Rancho Santa Fe unless they were servants.

* * *

As in so many places, the land tells the history. But we couldn't see—didn't know—the Native people, the colonizers, the proselytizers, the developers, and the workers who had made it so: The Kumeyaay-Ipai, who knew and stewarded every plant, animal, and season. The first exploratory incursions by the Spanish. The brutal mission period, which irrevocably transformed the land and decimated its peoples. The relatively brief Mexican rancho period, before Anglo settlers insinuated themselves into the landholding *Californio* families and reduced them to relics of a romanticized past. And then the coming of the railroad conglomerates and Anglo developers, who cloaked their proprietary violence in romantic fantasies of "gentleman" farming and the Spanish past. The Santa Fe Land Improvement Company (SFLIC). Developer Ed Fletcher. SFLIC vice president, William Hodges. They imprinted their names on the landscape: Rancho Santa Fe (the "town" in which we lived). Fletcher Cove (the beach we went to most often). Lake Hodges (the lake ten miles inland where we once tried and failed to catch fish; where, as a teenager, I went with friends to try to see shooting stars; and where, in 2010, a seventeen-year-old female jogger was raped and murdered).

In the early 1900s, the SFLIC found the wood from the alien eucalyptus trees they had planted all over the former Osuna Ranch too soft to use for railroad tracks. By the 1920s, they had decided to convert the land into an exclusive housing development, an embodiment of the Spanish fantasy past. They consulted with Ed Fletcher, who would later be instrumental in developing neighboring, racially exclusive Solana Beach, and ended up working with architect Lilian Rice of the firm Requa and Jackson. Rice traveled to Spain and modeled the architecture of Rancho Santa Fe's "town" after rural villages in Spain. Instead of a village well, though, there was a gas station designed to look like a well. Instead of peasants, Rancho Santa Fe's developers sought to recruit wealthy, white, "family"- and leisure-oriented residents.

Ed Fletcher also leased some of the land to Chinese and Japanese farmers and, in historian Phoebe Kropp's words, "directed them to prove the effectiveness of the land for cultivating fruits and vegetables" (a trick that would be repeated twenty-some years later by the US government when it strategically incarcerated skilled Japanese American farmers on sparsely populated lands they wished to develop for agriculture).

In 1923, the farmers' leases expired, and California's recently passed alien land laws made it difficult for them to renew. The citrus groves Asian American farmers were forced to abandon later became a hallmark of Rancho Santa Fe's brand of luxurious country living. ("Such plans did not include Asian farmers," says Kropp.) Mexican and Native American workers contributed their expertise, too, and did the heavy lifting. But they–we–couldn't live there unless they (we) served a white person.

* * *

While the house was plain, its grounds were not: the backyard featured a long, rectangular pool accompanied by a floral-tiled fountain that spewed water from the cement mouth of a satyr. In front of the house, along the curved, gravel driveway, was a citrus grove with fifty fruit-bearing trees, a remnant of the SFLIC's hubristic experiments on the land.

Our parents bought the house because of the orange trees, or at least that's what they told us. The fifty citrus trees included Valencia and navel oranges, tangelos, Satsuma tangerines, Meyer lemons, and limes. (Another benefit, my father said, was that we could not see our neighbors, and they could not see us.)

To the roses and palm trees, our parents added pomelo trees, guava trees, night-blooming cereus (smuggled on an airplane from Taiwan by family friends), camellias. In the garden area, they planted yam leaves, garlic chives, and later, kale and chard. Kyoho grapevines wound across the trellis of the front entrance, shading low bushes of Formosa azaleas. When my grandparents came to stay with us, my grandmother spent long hours in the garden while my grandfather tended the orange grove.

We put crawfish, captured from the golf course creek, in the fountain. We drove to the beach and caught grunion during their nighttime mating runs, when the beach became alive with wriggling silver life.

Once, my grandfather killed a four-foot-long snake slithering close to the house with a shovel to the head; my brother kept its heavy, coiled body, still twitching, in a plastic bag in his room overnight. Coyotes left their scat on the front walkway and in the backyard, and great horned owls hooted and swooped at twilight from the hundred-foot stand of eucalyptus trees that loomed over our backyard. Another time, I found a dead bunny on the driveway, probably hit by a car but looking entirely pristine. Within minutes, though, its luminous black eyes were picked out by crows.

* * *

After my brother and I left for college, one after the other, I didn't come back with any regularity for twenty years to this house, to this land, to my parents (and my brother never really did). For me to come home, it took my father becoming terminally ill, me learning how to be present during his slow decline and subsequent death, and then after that, a renewed and transformed relationship with my mother, which grew with strength and beauty and joy through our shared love of my young child. Through him, she took care of me once again, and finally, I began to take care of her, too.

During the long months of the COVID-19 pandemic, the house and land brought us peace and renewal. Isolation became safety, room to breathe. The luxury to breathe, when so many could not, and still cannot, amidst this time of immeasurable suffering and murderous neglect.

☀ ☀ ☀

Now, my mother has decided to sell the house and, with it, the land. It is time. It's all too big for just her, and my brother and I can't—won't—move back with our families. We will leave some of my dad here—under the camellias, in the orange grove. The places he loved the most. The trees that nourished us with their fruit and beauty for more than thirty years might be bulldozed by the next owner. The perfume of the lemons, the tart sweetness of the Satsumas—these trees that have borne witness to four generations of our family—gone in an afternoon.

A couple is very interested. They write a letter. The husband owns a business. The wife is an expert equestrian and looks forward to bringing her horse to The Ranch. (I instantly see the orange grove uprooted for a horse stable.) The husband wants to be close to the golf course. They have two young sons. ("I worked so hard to make this house perfect for a family," my mother says.) They love The Ranch. I know they will fit in instantly, in a way we never did.

What is land when it is property?

We buy it (if we are among the fortunate). We sell it. We leave parts of ourselves in it. We move on and start all over again, until we are gone, too. And yet the land endures.

PARK PLACE MATERIAL: PRIVATIZATION, HOMEOWNERS ASSOCIATIONS, AND MY DOG

ELAINE LEWINNEK

The unusually large size of the "Keep Out" sign makes me want to go in. I follow the dirt track between stucco duplexes, into the middle of the block, past a tire swing, out across the street to the middle of a bigger block, where paths meander beside a riverbed that has carved a small canyon. This is my suburban neighborhood's private park, twenty acres of open, rolling land that must have been too steep and too wet to build on when a developer constructed housing around it in 1976.

There are oddly tilted paths, not designed by any park expert, leading past grassy fields, an RV parking lot, sandstone outcroppings, cement-lined water culverts, a volleyball court, two baseball diamonds, and the remnants of kids' Nerf gun battles. Children, joggers, and birdwatchers follow the discreet paths into this hidden park, but most of the park's users are dog walkers. One of my neighbors reports that she has been scolded for walking in Park Place without a dog. The many shade trees remind me of my East Coast home, although one rainy day, I see teenagers surfing the slippery hills here, in a scene that can only be Californian, especially after the teens generously offer to share their surfboards with my young children, sliding down the muddy hills, laughing.

It's not just the surprisingly kind surfing teens that make this different from my Massachusetts home: my home did not have private parks. There were private golf courses on the other side of town, where kids cooler than me held clandestine keg parties. I recall adults showing me one or two tiny patches of private grass behind diminutive wrought-iron fences in the oldest parts of Boston and New York City, but those were archaic curiosities that looked boring to me. There were not a lot of private homeowners associations (HOA) in my part of New England. We had public town greens, public schoolyards, public hiking trails, public pools, and mostly public lakes, because the supposedly private ones were easy enough to sneak into, at least for white suburban kids like me.

When I first moved here and talked to my Orange County students about public space, one asked, "Who would want the public? The public means homeless people, strangers, maybe crowds with picket signs, rioting." I was a new teacher, new to a county famous for its conservatism, and I did not yet know how to encourage my diverse students to express their range of opinions. I hesitated to ask them whether they considered themselves "the public" and our classroom one form of "public space."

Instead I asked, "Where do you go when you want to collectively protest the latest act of police brutality?" Huntington Beach has its pier, Santa Ana has Sasscer Park / Black Panther Park, and Anaheim residents have held protests at their police headquarters, but what about the rest of suburban Southern California? I see people holding picket signs at highway entrance ramps or in Target parking lots. I live in Encinitas, where city hall is tucked away, out of sight. Only recently have some creative protesters laid claim to our goofy seaside surfing statue, the Cardiff Kook.

That early group of my students did not seem interested in protest sites. One of them explained the reason succinctly: "The public is smelly." I tried to tell the class that the public is not just protesters or unhoused individuals: it's anyone who wants to encounter people they have not explicitly planned to meet. It's me, for instance, looking for a space to walk my dog.

My dog is extremely social and impatient to be off-leash, desperate to run around with other dogs and other humans, too. After I discover the private Park Place Canyon, my dog and I start sneaking in almost every day. My dog cannot read the signs that tell her to keep out. She does not know to avoid the elderly guard who is paid minimum wage to keep her out. She runs up to him and leans against his knees, cuddling enthusiastically, lifting her head in adoration, blissfully unaware how clearly she is revealing that she lacks the distinctive dog tag issued only to residents of Park Place who have filled out the paperwork and paid the extra fee.

The guard pets my dog. Eventually, he chats with me, too. Robert doesn't like most people, but he loves dogs and they love him, and he seems to have decided that his job is to kick out the troublemakers, not me or my dog. He tells me when the coyotes are nesting or bees are swarming in Park Place Canyon. When the owls have babies, Robert knows which tree they are in, and loans me his binoculars to help me see the improbably majestic fluffballs. He spends a lot of mornings shooing the crows away from the baby owls, grumbling that the owl parents should pay better attention.

There are few fences or gates around this private park, so the dogs inside are fairly

well-behaved: no one trusts an out-of-control dog here. It's not a fortress-like gated community. It's not especially elite, either. In *Holy Land*, his memoir of suburban Lakewood, California, D.J. Waldie writes: "He thought of them as middle-class even though 1,100-square-foot tract houses on streets meeting at right angles are not middle-class at all." Park Place's largest homes are 922 square feet. Its duplexes and condos are modestly sized, though coastal California real estate values mean they are no longer modestly priced.

Robert notices when my dog is limping and advises me to put medicine on the scrape, then use a rubber band to secure an infant sock on that paw until it heals. It works. When my dog ages out of her submissive childhood and starts growling at some other dogs, Robert tells me which dogs to avoid in the canyon and teaches me how to rub my dog's shoulder to cure her anxiety.

Robert sleeps in his van, but the Park Place Homeowners Association does not allow him to park his van in their canyon when he is not at work, so every evening, after his shift is done, he drives forty-five minutes to a quiet parking lot where he spends his nights. He brings his dog Nala to work, but the Park Place HOA occasionally takes offense and declares Nala is not allowed, because Robert is not a resident of Park Place. I am not a resident of Park Place either, so I have no say.

There are more than eight hundred homes in Park Place, enough so the actual residents rarely realize that I don't belong. I look like them: white, middle-aged, dressed in athleisure. Our kids go to public school together, just across from their private park. I know their dogs' names. Some dogs have nearly human names (Leo, Jaimie, Maya, Annie, Stewie), some have food names (Cocoa, Maple, Chip), and a few have the names of gods (there are two Odins in this park).

It feels like an achievement when someone quietly informs me that Cocoa's owner is collecting a Christmas bonus for Robert. Robert has four kids from before his divorce, so they gather Robert's annual Christmas tip before December 1, because they want him to have extra cash to be able to buy presents for his children. After two years of invading this private park, I feel included—and bewildered that some people are sensitive enough to consider Robert's Christmas finances, while others don't even want his gentle sheepdog walking the park with him.

"It's not whether you live in Park Place, really," one man tells me. "It's whether your dog is Park Place material. And yours is." We had been strolling while our dogs romped, and this man had been telling me stories about hijinks at his first job, forty years ago, when he worked in a restaurant's kitchen, but suddenly he is speaking as if this park were an elite private school, as if my imperfect, usually enthusiastic, sometimes growly mutt had earned her way in. My dog is one of those dogs who smile. I smile. We pass.

Then Robert is fired. Someone on the HOA board wanted him to do more to keep out the likes of me. Someone else was upset that, after her husband died, Robert came to her door with a bouquet of flowers. She perceived this as flirtatious, and it made her uncomfortable to see Robert outside of the canyon. Like a plant out of place, Robert suddenly seemed like a weed. Others never liked his van or his dog. I don't have a say in any of this, of course. I also don't get to ask why the HOA overwaters the grass here, or why they keep removing the kids' zip lines and rope swings. I never even learned Robert's last name. I don't see him again.

The next two guards they hire are also fired, for sleeping in their cars when they are supposed to be guarding the canyon. No one else knows where the baby owls are, and I don't see them again either. The HOA finally finds a guard who will walk around, aggressively asking everyone for their dog tags. My kids beg me to stop going into the canyon after this guard scolds us.

"How did you get special permission to come in?" the owner of one of the Odin-dogs asks me, and I don't know what to tell her, because I don't want to talk to her about white privilege or the history of HOAs. I don't think it will help me keep accessing this park.

This was Kumeyaay land, first. The Spanish invaded, then Mexico claimed it, and in 1854, San Diego's mayor, Juan Maria Osuna, approved his own application for an 8,824-acre land grant including this space. After US conquest in 1848, across California, Anglo squatters, new US taxes, the droughts of the 1860s, and long-drawn-out court disputes over Spanish and Mexican land titles led much of this state to shift from Latino owners to Anglos, just a generation or two after it had shifted from Indigenous land claims to Latino. Anglo settlers chipped around the edges of Rancho San Dieguito until the Osuna family finally sold their remaining land to the railway company in 1906. Flower farmers grew poinsettias near here, while, in the 1920s, some of America's first yogis held services at the Self-Realization Fellowship on the coast, one mile away. After World War II, military members moved to this neighborhood next to the flower gardeners and hippies.

In 1963, just when civil rights protesters were gaining access to public pools and public parks, Orange County developers designed a new type of private space. They called it a "townhouse-on-the-green" and a "Common Interest Development," and they had to personally lobby for federal mortgage insurance for their novel concept of the homeowners association. Researching my book, *A People's Guide to Orange County*, I learned that Continental Townhomes in Huntington Beach was the first HOA, quickly followed by the College Green development in Fullerton and Treehaven West in Tustin. By 1965, Orange County had 10,000 homes in HOA developments and the US Department of Housing and Urban Development published a how-to booklet, *Planned-Unit Development with a Homes Association*, including sample legal documents. My college's library still has a copy.

The booklet explains that there is a need for urban densities with "a suburban feeling," planned around privately managed parks or pools. Because of the shared spaces held in common, an HOA community can have three times the residential density as another community with similar amenities, which means it has the potential for three times the profit for the developer. Earlier, most suburban developers who built parks or pools had turned them over to the public, not wanting the hassle of managing these spaces—but the 1965 booklet asserts that HOAs are not much work for developers and adds that public space "may encourage heavy public use which can adversely affect the residents of the subdivision [and] would undercut one of the principal attractions of the planned-unit concept." In the mid-1960s, during the civil rights movement, the public did not feel suburban.

HOAs require monthly fees while enforcing rules designed to present an image that is assumed to boost property values. Residents usually cannot place signs other than "For Sale," cannot choose what color to paint the outside of their homes, cannot hang laundry outdoors to dry, cannot leave their garage doors open, and cannot modify their home's exteriors without permission. The neighborhood's resale value is more important than the individual owner's varied desires to use their space. As Evan McKenzie explained in his classic 1994 book *Privatopia*, some HOA rules seem to limit free speech and freedom of assembly, but California's courts have generally decided that HOAs are business entities, not governments, and the courts assume that residents have voluntarily chosen these rules.

By 2010, half the housing in Orange County came with mandatory HOA membership, so many residents have little choice. Nor do they have democratic safeguards: HOA voting is typically limited to one vote per household, not one vote per adult, and renters are often disenfranchised, while rule changes are permitted only with a super-majority of seventy-five percent of all owners, not just seventy-five percent of those voting. By 2010, Orange County's HOAs collected more than $1 billion a year in fees, money that might otherwise have been public taxes paying for public parks available to all, but instead is directed to these privatized communities for a few. This may be why some of my students don't value public space.

Yet there is another California tradition for land use, too. Woody Guthrie traveled to California just before he wrote "This Land Is Your Land," including the often forgotten last verse:

> There was a big high wall there that tried to stop me.
> The sign was painted, said "Private Property."
> But on the backside, it didn't say nothing.
> This land was made for you and me.

I keep walking my dog.

CIMA DOME, EAST MOJAVE NATIONAL PRESERVE

RUTH NOLAN

AFTER THE DOME FIRE, AUGUST 2020

It's a hot, late September day, and I'm driving alone into the East Mojave Preserve from the south, following Kelso Road off of Interstate 40.

I'm on my way to view the impacts of the recent, devastating 43,000-acre Dome Fire, which ripped through the Cima Dome area, formerly home to one of the world's healthiest and most stunning Joshua tree woodlands.

I'm not intimidated by these vastly remote spaces of the Mojave Desert. In fact, I feel quite at home. Every mile I drive, past granite outcrops, ragged rock peaks, the massive Kelso Dunes, brings me closer to the heart of memory and home.

This is where I worked on many wildfires during the late 1980s, based at the Bureau of Land Management California Desert District Apple Valley Fire Station, a two-hour drive to the south. I worked one season on Engine Crew 6365 and a second season as a Helicopter 554 helitack/hotshot crew member.

As the miles melt into one another on this lonely, two-lane road, I'm embraced by memories that are both reassuring and unsettling as I remember firefighting moments and memories from time spent and shared with family and friends in subsequent years.

This is where I fell in love with my daughter's father, when we both worked on the engine crew. This is where we battled several vehicle fires and stopped the spread of any adjacent brush fires, using water hoses from our fire engine and the occasional shovel and chainsaw.

This is where I flew many times during the summer of 1987 on Helicopter 554, dropped off with six other crew members, high in the Granite Mountains to control a lightning-torched blaze in a pinyon pine forest and spend a surprisingly cold night to make sure the fire was completely out.

Every desert fire, past and present, especially ones I worked on, feels deeply personal to me, even now. As I watched media coverage of the Dome Fire play out online, I reacted as I usually do during every major desert fire event. I was frustrated and felt displaced to not be there in person, doing something to help with fire suppression operations—shovel work cutting fire line, perhaps, or helping at the makeshift helicopter operations base.

In particular, the East Mojave Preserve—a large part of my firefighter turf for two fire seasons—feels like home to me. My memories are seared into the landscape itself, so much so that I feel a lingering physical presence. With every new fire, I get a familiar rush of adrenaline, a huge responsibility to be there, participating in the teamwork and makeshift firefighter community to help mitigate the damage from the burn. Many of my former desert wildland firefighter friends tell me they react the same way.

There are the ruts of the Old Mojave Road heading west toward a harsh area known as the Devil's Playground, route for many nineteenth century pioneers heading west to the promised land of California citrus and sunshine, layered over a centuries-old trail established and used by Indigenous people traveling across the Mojave from one rare and precious water source to the next: places like Marl and ZZYZX Springs, often up to thirty miles apart. My daughter—now a young adult raising a family of her own in Minneapolis—and I explored out here in my Jeep years ago to search for and photograph thirty different species of desert wildflowers for her high school biology class project.

I drive past the Kelso Depot, a historic train station that's been recently refurbished to its early twentieth century glory, and head north toward Cima Road. In the west, I begin to see the massive bulge of Cima Dome, a part of the area out here known as the Cinder Cones National Natural Landmark. The remains of eroding granite that formed under the earth's surface millions of years ago, it rises 1,500 feet (460 m) above the volcanic plain and covers seventy square miles.

It is the color of charcoal today. The size of the Dome Fire slowly reveals itself, and the searing impact of its black wrath is obvious. Teutonia Peak, once covered with part of one of the world's most expansive Joshua tree forests, has taken on the tones and look of a cinder cone.

As I slow the car and pull into the small dirt parking area at the trailhead to Teutonia Peak, I look up: a red-tailed hawk circles above, riding on a fit of ash-strewn wind that is spinning into a dark dust devil.

I shift the car into park, turn off the ignition. Complete silence. I'm in a desert graveyard, and the most obvious dead appear to be the ghosts of charred Joshua trees.

My mind goes into a sort of firefighter mode as I begin to walk through the ashy remains, grateful I wore my oldest hiking boots, which are already getting charred. I imagine how this fire played out, what it would have been like to have worked on the Dome Fire.

I was, and still am, often asked why, as a woman, I would "do that kind of work." And to me, it's always been simple: it is work that I have felt incredibly at home with, at one with a working family, a job that has allowed me to express my love and need to nurture and care for the land that I deeply love. A perfect fit for me: tending to wildfire and observing its immediate and enduring impacts on the land.

Foremost is a feeling of performing a job that is layered in domestic terminology and structure. The firefighting community is as tightly knit and mutually interdependent as any strong family unit, crew members whose lives depend on the vigilance and support of one another.

Even many of the terms in the firefighter's lexicon are domestic: there's the endless chore known as "mopping up," which involves spending many slow and tedious hours walking through areas that have burned, stirring and cooling layers of hot ash. There are the times we'd spend "babysitting a fire," usually at night, when many blazes tended to slow down; the fire crew "laid itself down," where the team would spread themselves ten or twenty feet apart along a fire line at the edge of the burn to prevent spot fires from starting up in the green vegetation. And the activities that include "putting a fire to bed": wrapping up a wildfire event with a fire under control and operations winding down. There are also the "widow-makers", trees that have partially burned or whose roots are smoldering occasionally fall down without warning as crews work below. Sometimes that was lethal.

Even though I wasn't a mother yet, I operated in mama bear mode, without hesitation, ready to protect life and limb of my beloved desert and western wildlands, as well as human lives and homes.

We were firmly guided by critical principles, such as the Ten Basic Firefighter Rules, imprinted on my brain to this day and often a guiding survival template in day-to-day living that has informed my work as a parent and educator in so many ways. For example: Be alert, keep calm, think clearly, and act decisively. Know your escape route at all times. Give clear instructions, and ensure they are understood. Fight fire aggressively, having provided for safety first.

I'll never forget the scorching summer day working on a desert fire when a crew member, a friend to this day, turned and yelled, "Rattlesnake!" just as I was about to step on a huge Mojave Green.

I learned, through vivid and immediate experience, that sometimes, fires are mostly out of firefighters' control. That things don't always turn out the way we would have expected them to. And that we have to learn to live with that. We can't save everything. And firefighters sometimes get injured. Some even die.

As I walk along the edge of the ragged, hastily cut fire line at the edge of the burn zone, I search for what firefighters may have left behind: boot prints in the ashes, not erased away by rain; fragments of charred fire hose; perhaps a broken boot lace or someone's crumpled bandana. I can almost hear the whine of Helicopter 554's rotors and feel the wash of wind and sting of dirt kicking up in my face as I guide it to land for another water bucket refill, a gritty taste in my mouth.

The jagged caw-caw of a raven perched atop a black bristle of burnt Joshua tree pulls me out of my reverie. I look to the sky, which is slowly turning into a hazy brown as smoke from multiple other wildfire events across California and the western US works its way across the Mojave.

As I survey the hulking charred ruins of the Joshua tree forests stretching beyond me farther than I can see, I can't help but wonder, like a fretful parent soothing their little one's feverish brow while trying to work out how their child has gotten seriously ill: what happened out here? Why and how did this desert fire get so big? Why did it take four days for helicopter support?

It's a tragedy that the Dome Fire grew to the size it did. It's inexplicable to me that H554 didn't get out here as an initial attack crew and get this fire under control immediately. I know it was possible, had resources been available on August 1 when a lightning strike started this blaze. Then again, there were so many things out of anyone's control that day. Fire resources were already stretched thin as multiple major fires played out across California, an unfortunate situation worsened by the sharp reduction of available inmate firefighter crews due to the coronavirus pandemic.

I'm reminded, as I look for signs of life and recovery and don't see any yet, that many expectations in my personal life haven't turned out the way I thought they would.

It wasn't long after my time working on fires out here that my daughter's father began his lifelong stints in prison—first working for Susanville fire camp, and later, as his crimes became more serious, time in maximum security prison. I haven't communicated with him in years.

My boyfriend, ten years ago, dying by suicide not long after we took our beauty-love drive through here and added to the stories. My friend, who I collected soil samples with and bonded over our appreciation for the nuances of how to get unstuck from deep sand, died several years ago in a terrible highway accident.

And so it is that I stand alone out here, embraced in a collective grief that is not mine alone. I also share it with many friends and desert lovers who use social media to express their dismay at the Joshua tree loss.

It's awkward that the trees are still here. They still stand, and many will soon tumble to the ground, their limbs strewn across a suddenly emptied land like human bones, and the recovery in this arid land will evolve slowly, the way all ecologies in the desert do, like the movements of a desert tortoise. And fire regimes—long-term burn and recovery impacts and adaptations/regrowth in Mojave Desert ecologies are still not entirely known.

But standing in loss is not enough. What will I tell my grandchildren when I bring them here?

Fire, one of the four basic elements, even at its most terrible, works its magic in the desert in ways we do not understand. I have enough knowledge from experience to know that fire on the land is both a blessing and a bane, and I'm nourished by my growing understanding, layered atop my firefighting work and my ongoing research for my humanities project, *Fire on the Mojave: Stories from the Deserts and Mountains of Inland Southern California*, that beauty and restoration will come.

So many desert stories, mine, by those who passed through here before me, and by those I worked alongside on fire crews. Today, I'm bound to honor these stories and keep their visages alive, just as the Joshua trees have not simply disappeared—they have been transformed, even if that transformation is not what I want to see.

I refuse to resign myself to the circulating, apocalyptic idea that climate change has destroyed this place forever. That at the whim of a lightning strike and a resulting massive fire fueled by climate change alone, this cherished and well-tended place has turned into an eternal place of death.

I'll bring my little grandchildren here next spring, and as with other Mojave Desert wildfire remains, we'll look for places on this altered landscape that may have been obscured before the fire. Perhaps we'll find sleeping circles or petroglyphs on the rocks at one of the area's springs, now revealed after the underbrush has been burned away. We may even discern—and follow—the faint traces of forgotten trails, where so many of our ancestors have walked before us.

And if we come at the right time, whether or not there has been adequate winter rain, we'll surely see wildflowers carpeting the burn zone with purple, yellow, white, and orange, a direct result of the fire. A vivid display occurred after the 2005 Hackberry Fire, as well as native shrubs resprouting. We may even see the tiniest of resprouts of some Joshua trees, needling their way toward the sun, one slow but sure inch at a time.

I'll bring a stack of makeshift fire tools—small, foldable shovels—to teach the kids how to cut a small fire line, how to stir the ashes and make sure the hot coals are completely out, and how to work as a team. We will learn how to tend the land by fighting fire, even if it's make-believe for them, how to care for our desert land, together, as a family. Together, we will build relationships with wildfire and the long-established fire ecologies here in the Mojave Desert, where fires will inevitably burn, part of the natural processes of lightning and flame and transformation spelled out upon the land.

LOOKING TO THE SKY IN THE ANTELOPE VALLEY

LISA COVERT

When I saw the news that test pilot Charles "Chuck" Yeager died on December 7, 2020, I was transported back to my childhood in California's Antelope Valley, where he famously broke the sound barrier. The Antelope Valley of the 1980s and 1990s, when I was growing up, was a mostly unremarkable place. Joshua trees and golden poppies added a touch of beauty to the otherwise sepia-toned expanse, but over the years, housing tracts consumed more and more of their desert habitat. For many residents, the small cities and unincorporated areas in the vast stretch of the Mojave Desert where Los Angeles, Kern, and San Bernardino Counties meet were an affordable place to call home after long commutes to and from Los Angeles, which my family called "down below."

But the Antelope Valley had a very important claim to fame: aerospace. It was the gateway to Edwards Air Force Base (formerly Muroc Air Force Base), the NASA Dryden Flight Research Center, and the Rocket Research Laboratory, commonly referred to as the "Rocket Site." Closer to home we had Plant 42, an Air Force facility that was utilized by the who's who of the aerospace industry: enormous hangars run by Northrop Grumman, Boeing, Lockheed Martin, and Rocketdyne towered over the flat desert landscape. Sometimes, when you were driving by, the huge doors would be open and you could catch a glimpse inside. Everyone who lived in the valley knew someone in the industry or at the base. My father, a welder, had jobs at Edwards, the Rocket Site, and Plant 42 over the years, when he wasn't commuting "down below."

In the prologue to the 1990 bestseller *City of Quartz*, Mike Davis described the Antelope Valley as a "militarized desert" and "the Pentagon's playground." Davis's assessment, suggesting a dystopian future, resonates with my historian's sense of the present. But it was not how I saw things when I was growing up. Back then, the term "aerospace" had an aspirational ring to it that minimized the military side of things. The focus instead was on science and technological advancement. One of the region's most notable distinctions was that it was the first landing site for the space shuttle *Columbia* in 1981, just months after I was born. Edwards Air Force Base served as one of only three shuttle landing sites in the country. Its arid climate and expansive lake bed known as Rogers Dry Lake made for a relatively predictable runway.

We were trained to look to the sky. I remember being ushered outside in the hopes of seeing the space shuttle during my childhood (which, according to NASA, landed at Edwards forty-five times while I was living in the Antelope Valley). Perhaps this is why one of my earliest memories is watching the space shuttle *Challenger* explode on TV in 1986 when I was five years old. Aerospace, its hopes and its dangers, was deeply embedded in our local culture.

Test pilots were our local heroes, commemorated by an Aerospace Walk of Honor on Lancaster Boulevard, which since 2000 has also been graced by a thirty-foot-long mural of Chuck Yeager. My middle school was named after test pilot and astronaut Joe Walker; our mascot was the Jets. Pilot and astronaut William "Pete" Knight converted his aerial accomplishments into political currency, serving as city council member (1984–1988) then mayor (1988–1992) of the City of Palmdale, and later as the district's representative in the California State Assembly (1992–1996) and Senate (1996–2004). A mosaic celebrating the aerospace industry adorned the Lancaster Home Savings Bank. Generations of local debutantes, including my mother and myself and my sisters, were escorted by Air Force cadets flown in from Colorado Springs for an annual valley-wide ball.

Aerospace culture in the Antelope Valley was an opportunity to be a part of something bigger, to explore the vast expanses of the universe, to be on the cutting edge of technology. I had poor eyesight and never really enjoyed math, so aerospace wasn't a calling for me. My sister did experiment with it in the late 1990s and early 2000s, first as a cadet in the local Civil Air Patrol, and then as a participant in NASA's Summer High School Apprenticeship Research Program at Edwards Air Force Base. These opportunities helped show a girl with Mexican American heritage that the sky was the limit, or perhaps better put, that there was no limit to what she could do. But her eventual career in civil engineering and development was more closely tied to the land.

Chuck Yeager was famous for being the first person to break the sound barrier in 1947, and he did it flying over Rogers Dry Lake. It sounds like a metaphor, to "break the barrier," but when you feel the resultant sonic boom, it makes sense. Sonic booms are tangible; they rattle windows and reverberate through the earth. I can't explain the physics of it, but the vast openness of the desert seemed to amplify the booms. Sonic booms were a relatively normal occurrence in the Antelope Valley, another reason to look up. If you were lucky, you would see the latest in aerospace technology being tested in the skies. I grew up knowing the names of these aircraft, the F-117 Nighthawk, the SR-71 Blackbird, and the B-2 Spirit or B-2 Stealth Bomber. These projects were shrouded in secrecy, so when the B-2 Stealth Bomber was publicly unveiled in the Antelope Valley in 1988 to much fanfare, as a seven-year-old I felt privileged to have a metaphorical front row seat.

When I heard about Chuck Yeager's death, my childhood proximity to "aerospace" had already been on my mind, prompted by a friend's social media post about sonic booms the day before. I currently live in Charleston, South Carolina, which in most respects feels light years away from the desert landscape of my childhood. It is a lush, green coastal city that averages approximately six times the annual rainfall of the Antelope Valley. But we have our own air force base, Joint Base Charleston, and even though it is not home to a flight-testing facility, military planes are not uncommon in our local skies. Occasionally, we hear sonic booms. I have honestly never paid much attention since I have lived here, in part because the foliage makes it more difficult to track planes across the sky. So it was jarring when my friend, who was raised in Beirut during the Lebanese Civil War, posted that "Hearing military airplanes and the breaking of the sound barrier" was triggering for her. My first impulse (bad as they often are on social media) was to comment on how it was such a normal part of my childhood. Fortunately, I exercised restraint. I realized it was a normal part of hers too, but on the receiving end. Whereas my childhood experience in the 1980s and 1990s was being able to witness America's extraordinary ingenuity and technological accomplishments, she lived on the other side of those "advances." I cannot remember whether, as a child, I ever wondered what or who the bombers were actually designed to bomb. I cannot say with certainty that those specific technologies tested in my backyard were utilized in that conflict. But the juxtaposition was nonetheless a jolt to my consciousness.

I grew up in a world where the Cold War was supposedly cold, where the B-2's stealth technology was designed to outsmart Soviet anti-aircraft technology, where the nearby San Andreas fault line was the only real threat to the desert we called home. I did not understand that the Antelope Valley was such a significant part of the military-industrial complex, that is, until I began to study history in college. However even then, I did not fully connect the dots between the hometown heroes like Chuck Yeager and death and destruction in other parts of the world. Even the space program, which as a child seemed benign and wondrous, had military implications that I did not consider until much later.

Activity at the base and testing sites has declined since the Cold War heyday and the end of the shuttle program in 2011. Aerospace contractors have shifted production to places with cheaper labor, including South Carolina. However, the late 1990s ushered in a new era of testing unmanned aircraft that became signature technologies in our forever wars in Afghanistan, Iraq, and other distant places we do not acknowledge on the nightly news. More recently, Edwards has served as a testing site for private-public space collaborations including the Jeff Bezos-funded Blue Origin lunar lander project, Blue Moon.

Reflecting back on my childhood, one of the things that is most striking was the ease of complicity in the military-industrial complex. The label "aerospace" helped sanitize the true purposes for the many innovations that were built and tested in

these spaces. But the term itself was not enough to keep the Antelope Valley clean. A 2017 ProPublica study identified, for example, more than three hundred hazardous waste sites on and surrounding Edwards Air Force Base, a reminder that the aerospace industry did not just cause harm in the places where bombs were dropped, but also left a legacy of harm for the communities that supported it.

I have not lived in the Antelope Valley since I graduated high school in 1999, but I return regularly to visit family. My middle school has been rechristened the Joe Walker STEALTH Academy (Science, Technology, Engineering, And Learning Through Humanities) with a new logo emblazoned with the Stealth bomber. But more generally, it seems the reverence for aerospace culture and test pilots has somewhat diminished with the advent of unmanned flights, the elimination of the Space Shuttle program, and the passing of Chuck Yeager's generation. The City of Lancaster ended its Aerospace Walk of Honor program in 2009, perhaps a sign of the times. Recent controversies about the costs of the failed F-35 fighter jet have renewed conversations about our nation's bloated defense budget. I don't know if the Antelope Valley has new heroes now. My hope is that we can look forward to a time when we can all look to the skies with joy and wonderment, and that the militarized desert can find a new claim to fame.

160 MILES EAST OF LOS ANGELES: ON COVERING THE EASTERN COACHELLA VALLEY

RUXANDRA GUIDI

There's this hill, a perfectly sloped green hill, that rises above the Pomona Freeway on your left as you cross the 605 and drive west into Los Angeles. Young trees stand equidistant from one another—clearly planned and planted not long ago. Between them, snaking their way from street level all the way up to the top mesa, green plastic tubes, about two feet in diameter, rise above the ground, transporting the methane gas produced by the slowly decomposing trash that lives inside the belly of the mountain.

As the population of Los Angeles County has expanded over the last fifty years, so has the hill. About a decade ago, an average 12,000 tons of trash arrived daily (that's the equivalent of about two hundred adult elephants, to give you an idea) atop these huge dump trucks. The non-recyclable waste would then get flattened out by the dump truck's equally huge wheels. I had a photo taken next to one of them just so I could remember their size: a bright yellow safety helmet sits awkwardly atop my head; behind me, one of the truck's tires rises to twice my size.

"All waste facilities have great views," one of the landfill's workers told me back in 2010 when I visited Puente Hills. He pointed down to cookie-cutter housing developments, a few pockets of green, and orderly suburban streets where cars could be seen shuttling in all directions and at different speeds.

But a mountain of trash is still trash, no matter how many trees may be covering it up, no matter how pretty the sight. And this perfectly sloped mountain of trash was getting to be just too big for Los Angeles. The Puente Hills landfill would have to close down, and the trash would need to be shipped elsewhere.

* * *

Early one summer, a little over a decade ago, my editor sent me to a town about 160 miles east of Los Angeles. My assignment was to spend a couple of days trying to understand why there had been a history of illegal dumping in these parts, and why the Los Angeles County Sanitation District had considered the Imperial Valley desert close to the US–Mexico border a future disposal site.

I took Interstate 8 east of San Diego, toward the Jacumba Mountains' huge, round boulders, past a border patrol checkpoint, and the curve in the road that brought me just a mile away from the US–Mexico border wall. Then, less than two hours into my ride past another rocky mountain range, the plain opened up in front of me just as the sun was coming up. I could see just two layers in the landscape ahead—the Imperial Valley's sandy light brown and a blue sky—that resembled a Mark Rothko painting.

The closer I got to my destination, the more green mixed into the landscape. This is the Eastern Coachella desert but still it is known for its agricultural production 300 days of the year, only made possible by an informal migrant workforce and intense irrigation. Eighty-eight percent of cropland here is artificially irrigated with water from the All-American Canal.

Seasonal farm workers can be seen dotting the fields and picking produce almost year-round, even when temperatures reach 110 degrees. By the time I showed up to the unincorporated community of Thermal mid-morning, the air was dry and warm. Eduardo Guevara, a gentle, stocky guy with a closely cropped dark mustache and beard, waited for me by the side of the road.

I first heard about Lawson Dump when I became obsessed with Los Angeles's massive output of trash and wondered where it ends up. It turned out some of the county's construction debris and hazardous waste was illegally ending up here, a fifty-foot-high dump that would be set on fire regularly. Next to it was Duroville, a trailer park infamous for its poor living conditions and bad air quality. Without paved roads and garbage pickup, Duroville was a sad indictment of the daily reality of too many California farmworkers. And it was overcrowded—at one point, up to 4,000 people lived on the forty-acre site.

Activist Eduardo Guevara took a picture inside Lawson Dump as smoke rises from a fire smoldering below ground. Although it was ordered closed in 2006, underground fires continued to burn for years afterward, and residents of nearby mobile home parks continued to complain about noxious odors and possible contamination.

Meanwhile, Duroville residents had no idea of the possible risks of living next to a smoldering dump. "This is where nearby farms disposed of grape stakes covered in pesticides, where people discarded their old cell phones and computers," Eduardo told me as we walked around the edge of the dump. "We knew people burned trash here, but we didn't know it was that bad."

Even before coming to Thermal, I'd become both fascinated and repelled by this place: here was the largest toxic dump in California located a short drive east from the gated communities and irrigated golf courses of Palm Springs and the site of the Coachella music festival. It was a symbol of the great disparities you'd find in the state: of the migrant farmworker as a dispensable asset, of the desert landscape as a literal wasteland.

We spent much of that day exploring the four unincorporated rural towns of the Eastern Coachella Valley that border the Salton Sea: Thermal, Mecca, Oasis, and North Shore. Eduardo told me he'd managed to get his family out of a trailer, but his wife still suffered from the severe asthma she acquired during their time in Duroville. He'd begged county officials to do something about poor quality housing, pesticide drift, hazardous waste, and water contamination, but nothing came of it.

"Maybe researchers couldn't link the asthma directly to the dumps, but it's a big coincidence for a community that has been living next to a burning, open-air dump for years, don't you think?" he said, as we stood atop one of the mounds that made up Lawson Dump. I listened to him intently, thinking I'd also need to get a response from public officials, check the record, do my research, be objective. My story, I genuinely thought, would capture the injustices of this place. It would take me some time—years, really—to be able to identify the lessons that this part of the desert held for me.

I kept coming back, driving the two-and-a-half to three hours from the city. By 2014, the Los Angeles County Sanitation District decided to indefinitely postpone its "waste-by-rail" plans of moving LA's trash to this part of the state and Lawson Dump was ordered shut by a court. More often than not, I came alone and without an assignment, struggling to make a case to my editor that one or two stories couldn't possibly capture the complexity of what I was seeing or what it all meant.

☀ ☀ ☀

I met Griselda Barrera at a middle school auditorium in Thermal, moments after she offered her public comment about air quality to a panel of state regulators. With her long, black hair, straight talk, and black platform pumps, Griselda demanded attention. But the public officials facing her, all of them men, avoided her gaze.

"I'm tired of the agencies that come here asking us to bring people from the community as an audience for their presentations," she said out loud in Spanish. "We have no idea what they do with the information we give them. Nothing changes."

Fifteen years ago, Griselda told me, she and her family came from Mexico and moved into Duroville. They, of course, hated it. She and her husband got a seasonal job picking grapes and *chiles*, averaging only $15,000 per year.

Low wages in the fields define this corner of California: they are the reason why a majority of workers endure substandard living conditions in mobile home parks, and why at the height of harvesting season, four men will share a single room for months, or worse yet, live out of their cars. Income inequality is why migrant

populations typically are forced to face extreme levels of environmental hazards and also why migrants' health disparities are so persistently widespread. In 2010, there was only one primary care physician per every 8,400 residents in the Eastern Coachella Valley. Local clinics report higher rates of diabetes and asthma, particularly among young children, coupled with a thirty percent uninsured rate among patients.

"I'm taking you to the new Duroville," Griselda promised me the day we met, explaining how after the old dump and trailer park had been ordered shut down, the county created a new $28 million public-private mobile home development in its stead. I'd be able to meet Griselda's youngest son who'd dropped out of college and now worked in a fast food joint, and her eldest, who had just welcomed a baby with his young wife from El Salvador who had also spent her first few years in America living in (but plotting her exit out of) Duroville.

"But you should think about a way to pay people for their time," Griselda said, coyly, as we made plans to meet again. I tried to explain to her that it was unethical for journalists to pay for interviews. Then, for weeks, I waited for Griselda to reply to my messages.

I was once a middle-class kid growing up in Caracas, Venezuela, a big city flanked by mountains and less than an hour's drive from the Caribbean Sea; an urban setting not unlike Los Angeles, located far away from where my food was grown and where my trash was disposed of.

The tropics' tall, flowering trees and seasonal monsoon rains defined my view of nature. When my family visited the desert dunes in Coro, 300 miles west of Caracas, we jokingly called it "a beach without water," a habitat for scorpions and snakes. I never thought I'd one day come to love the Eastern Coachella desert and the Sonoran Desert, my home of the past five years, with its stalwart and adaptable biodiversity despite high summer temperatures and a lack of water.

Once in the US, I would become an outsider: Spanish-speaking, but not from Mexico. Nostalgic, but increasingly independent and distant from my own family's traditions. I learned to survive winters.

The deeper I got into the legacies of Duroville and Lawson Dump, the more I learned about the life and work and dreams of migrant farmworkers, the harder it became to sort out whether I was being a well-meaning witness to injustice or someone exploiting the details of others' suffering for my own sake. It turns out that, like most journalists, I could be both.

Like a privileged Western foreign correspondent parachuted into a conflict area in the developing world, I was routinely asked to make sense of a history I did not feel or know. Yet for years, I'd functioned under the assumption that as a journalist, my craft was the only thing I needed to show loyalty to. My stories, I naively thought, would shed light on the injustices faced by people, creating a shift in public opinion and, eventually, tangible change.

It would take me another decade to see the shortsightedness of this promise—mainly, that I could efficiently yet deeply understand and share stories about "other" people and places, without getting to truly understand myself first. Neither my class consciousness nor my native Spanish-speaking could make up for the easy characterization of other people's lives, for the way their stories could be perceived by others, how they could contribute to the already existing stereotypes about migrants, desert-dwellers, immigrants, farm workers, activists.

I needed to sort out my duty to the people who trust me with their lives and feelings, and figure out that in the end, these stories I'm drawn to, past and present, are also about myself: They are stories about home or the search for it. Stories about dignity and justice. More often than not, the narratives I care to help tell the most, the ones that keep me up at night and give me a sense of purpose, are about individuals and communities who have a sense of hope about their futures.

In getting to know the desert—its vastness and possibility—I have learned to slow down my experiences to see what happens when I give myself one month or two or a year to tell a story, instead of one day or one week. Sometimes, the stories never get told and instead, I befriend the people I interview. Other times, these stories morph into life lessons instead or into yet more stories, or rather, snippets that make their way into my dreams. The places I write about become fixations, and I keep returning, as if hitting the rewind button to replay the scenes of a movie that hold some personal meaning that I cannot yet decipher.

This past November, I paid my latest visit to Thermal. Eduardo and Griselda are no longer living nearby, but the last time we spoke, they'd both told me how proud they were of the roles each of them played in the cleanup of the old Lawson Dump site. The hill is still there. It rises above street level but the waste is now hidden beneath thick layers of dirt. Next door, where Duroville's trailers once peppered the landscape, there is nothing but flat open land. Beyond, on either side, I could see a patchwork of fields of lettuce and other greens being harvested by men and women hunched forward, donning big hats, dreaming their dreams of home here in the desert, or elsewhere.

THE TIDES THAT ERASE: AUTOMATION AND THE LOS ANGELES WATERFRONT

JENNIFER CARR

Whenever I go out with my father anywhere in San Pedro, we inevitably run into someone he knows, from his school days (a long time gone), from the Cabrillo Beach Polar Bear Club, or from years of work spent on the harbor. That's when San Pedro, with a population of 56,000, feels like a small town.

My dad, now a retired longshore worker and marine clerk, Locals 13 and 63, remembers faces better than names, and a casual—someone who takes jobs out of the casual hall and isn't a steady at a particular dock—comes up to my dad as we sit down for burgers on Gaffey Street and asks, "Jack, you still down at Pasha Stevedoring?"

"Retired three years now," my dad says, and I can tell he's searching for the name to go with the face. But names don't always matter, because there are now two workers from the waterfront in one place, two brothers in the union, which means they can have a full conversation in the shared language of the docks.

The San Pedro Bay Port Complex, comprised of the combined ports of Los Angeles and Long Beach, makes up the ninth largest port in the world (the top eight are all in Asia). Realizing its potential value, Los Angeles annexed San Pedro as a part of the City of Los Angeles in 1909, and the complex has since been given the moniker (and a National Geographic Channel show along with it) *America's Port*, since it handles more than forty percent of all containerized cargo that enters the United States. However, this distinction has an uncertain future with the dredging and widening of the Panama Canal, the fully automated barge port in Louisiana, or the megaships that can carry over 20,000 twenty-foot equivalent unit containers. These container ships have a beam of about 193 feet—compared with the one hundred-foot bow-to-stern total length of the *San Salvador*, the flagship galleon of Juan Rodríguez Cabrillo, who in 1542 became the first European to scout the San Pedro Bay, inhabited by the Tongva, whose settlement in the bay was named Kiinkenga.

While waiting for our burgers, the longshore worker tells us, "I only get out three days a week now—work is down because of tariffs. There are no slabs at all." Because I'm the daughter of a former longshore worker/marine clerk, I know that slabs are hunks of steel made from ingots rolled out on a belt in lengths between thirteen and forty-four feet, weighing between ten and twenty-seven tons. I know that the 1960 Modernization and Mechanization Agreement enabled containerized cargo, a move that prevented the union from rejecting any future technological advancements in the port but simultaneously negotiated the union's ability to be trained on and operate the new technology. I know that my dad first got his start on the docks in 1959, just out of high school, and used a nine-inch metal hook to unload cargo onto pallets. I know the rhythms and the cadences of waterfront speak and its hopes and losses by heart.

The trade war is affecting everyone who isn't currently pulling a retirement pension or already in the ground. A trade war means fewer ships in the harbor, fewer gangs called up for a shift—"Only two gangs ordered per ship!" our new friend tells us while we wait for our burgers. "And only two foremen now each for the day and night shifts, when before there were five!" I see both my dad's relief at being out and guilt over getting the best deal out of his last contract before retirement.

Work on the waterfront has always been a tenuous balance between the members of the International Longshore and Warehouse Union—my dad's union—and the shipping companies represented by the maritime association. Bloody Thursday honors the flashpoint of the 1934 West Coast Waterfront Strike that involved scabs and hired goon squads beating up (and shooting) striking union members, killing two of them. It's now commemorated every July 5, with a harbor shutdown and branded t-shirts. In 1960, the Modernization and Mechanization Agreement meant that companies could containerize cargo, reducing physical labor, but that the union had to handle the movement and stowage from ship to dock. The union would have to be allowed the chance to modernize with the technology.

In 2002, there was the weeks-long lockout after the union was accused of a slowdown, during which the union leveraged its power to negotiate a favorable contract with the association representing the shipping companies (despite George W. Bush invoking the Taft Hartley Act as a means to weaken the union, attempting to render them unable to strike). In January of 2015, I marched alongside my dad and thousands of other ILWU families in support of the union's contract negotiations, and in 2019, the union rallied once again to protest shipping giant Maersk's addition of 130 robotic vehicles to replace human-operated machines to sort and move cargo on the docks. A lopsided agreement was made; though the union can be trained on the new automation, jobs will still be reduced, and the union has been leveled a devastating blow. It's not the Matrix or Skynet—but there's a real fear that in two generations, with

automation potentially replacing most of the workforce, there will be few who know what it meant to work on the waterfront. Reactions range anywhere on the spectrum between hysteria to excitement, depending on which side of the labor vs. management debate you're on.

As for now, we don't know what's going to happen. Maersk uses microchips in the containers and even on the docks, plugged into robots to do the work my father spent hours of his week planning out. He'd come home, dusted yellow with spray chalk from marking steel slabs and coils, marking the yard for placing the slabs, coils, and plywood to be loaded onto trucks or rail cars, double checking bills of lading, somehow sorting cargo the way a conductor guides a symphony or the Sorcerer Supreme bends the world to his will.

The waterfront is the true official language of San Pedro, which otherwise has been a pidgin of Spanish, English, Croatian, Italian, and Japanese since Juan Domínguez was given the land grant by Spain for ranching in 1784 (and the subsequent US takeover of California after the Mexican-American War). Phineas Banning, an immigrant from the East Coast, dredged the harbor in 1871 to make it deep enough for ships to pass through, and two years later, as California state senator, used government funds to build the first breakwater. My great-grandfather, an immigrant from Croatia (then the Austro-Hungarian Empire), found his way to San Pedro in 1914 in his purse seiner, *The Agram*, after freezing on the waters of Puget Sound. San Pedro looked similar to the Adriatic coast, Catalina Island a more distant Krk, the harbor town a larger iteration of Crikvenica and Rijeka. Familiarity and echoes of home bays and fishing communities drew most of the families that came to San Pedro during the twentieth century.

The stories of San Pedro are woven out of fishing nets, metal hooks, and family recipes. San Pedrans also retain their ties to cultural heritage—many of my friends still return to Croatia every summer—but even stronger is the Pedro heritage. Families remember who fished on the *Sea Scout* between 1950 and 1959, or how many owners the *John R.* had. The first boat my grandfather owned was also the first all-steel purse seiner on the coast, the *Paramount*. Starting in the 1930s, he spent months at a time off the Galapagos Islands fishing tuna, dropping off loads in Mexico, then motoring south again for another load. During World War II, he and the rest of the fishing fleet took turns patrolling the coast for submarines, then scooping up every last sardine and anchovy from the waters—whatever could be put in a can, stowed in musty holds, or shipped to the fronts. When the fishing dwindled, the men moved onshore, but not too far, from the boats to the docks, cargoes of bananas from Brazil, coffee from Colombia, sugar from Hawaii, cowhides from wherever it was the cowhides came from. Bales of cotton loaded on pallets, hand-stowed, hand-offloaded, hand-sorted, with steel hooks in the hand to move the pulleys, separate the loads, throw the cargo onto trucks or railcars.

Some symphonies are played with violins and cellos and flutes—my family created them with hooks and pallets and the rhythms of human automation, smooth, choreographed, memorized, inherited. Water is in our blood and our bones, and our steps pulse with the low hum of the cranes that lift and pull cargo the way the moon pulls the tides and the way we pull stories from salt.

San Pedrans are wary, not necessarily of progress, not necessarily of being left behind—although that is a concern—but worse, of being erased altogether.

There's a hole in my heart where Canetti's Seafood Grotto used to be, down in the throat of 22nd Street, tucked behind the fish markets. It was an archive that sold fish, but the real draw was the characters inside, human libraries reciting their daily litanies, rimes of not-so-ancient mariners who didn't measure days with coffee spoons but instead counted years by fishing boats. Who fished on which boat and with whom, who partnered, who owned outright, was it longlining tuna or nets of sardines or anchovies or *ligni*—squid—conjured to the surface of the ocean with spotlights. After my grandfather died, I worked at Canetti's for a time, absorbing the stories of other grandfathers, imbibing the sounds the way others who grieve sniff items of clothing. In the age of computer automation, this worked as a different kind of neural network, the individual stories binding us all in one greater story.

After sixty years, Canetti's closed up shop, the larger-than-life Joe Canetti retired, and like my grandfather and so many others, he is now gone, lost to the tides of time.

Canetti's fish tacos and sandwiches were famous, but my dad and I often switched up our orders to get their burgers, a greasy-spoon-diner-type of burger, and the closest we can replicate (though still aren't quite the same) we've tracked down to a sandwich shop on Gaffey Street. And here, just like at Canetti's, the pulse of the harbor carries us to another thread of the collective story of the waterfront.

The man at lunch on Gaffey Street mentions a name I know, says this worker got laid off because work was so slow, and now had to take jobs out of the casual hall. "And he's a good worker, too."

A good worker. Akin to the title of Sorcerer Supreme, it's the highest compliment you can give someone on the waterfront. Though it may sound Bolsheviky, the "good worker" plaudit is an apolitical mark of distinction that is carried down generations. At Canetti's, people could recall good workers who had been dead for ten or twenty years. Prime table position was given to Ray Patricio, one of the "best bosses" to ever work down at the harbor.

My dad is one of the good workers, a trait that imbued every part of his life. "You know how lucky you are?" his coworkers would tell me at holiday parties or the occasional run-in at Canetti's, the movie theater, the Target parking lot. My dad's vice president (on the management side) said on multiple occasions that he'd retire when my dad retired. When my dad did retire—at the age of seventy-five—two workers filled his position. Fifty-seven years he spent on the waterfront. Eight-, ten-, sometimes fourteen-hour days. In that time, he clocked in almost twenty orthopedic surgeries, his body given over wholly to the job.

Having a good worker in the family is a sense of pride. I didn't earn it, but it sticks to me, a benediction, a membership card for respect. It's the story that has framed my entire life, just like my grandfather's story framed my father's.

The port complex currently provides 190,000 jobs to human beings who pay taxes, buy homes, shop locally, send their kids to Little League and soccer. Automation will change the complexion of the entire town, and it's already changing. San Pedrans look around at places like this sandwich hangout on Gaffey Street, wondering which of us gentrification will bump off first. Without the language of the waterfront and the people who speak it, what will happen to the rest of the town? Losing this language is personal. It's akin to losing my grandfather all over again.

Now, perhaps, is the coda, but maybe not. Maybe as the workers shift to fit themselves into the narrower machinations, they'll forge new shapes and new rhythms that will be just as beautiful, though different, perhaps a little melancholic. The stories will go on, and there will be enough of us left who know even a few words of the old language to tell the stories of those who have come and gone: *break bulk, hooks, casual cards, A books, long on hours, a good worker, the best worker, my grandfather, my father, my father*. I repeat it like a prayer, a chronicle of what was, saying it often so there will be no end to the echo.

WE ARE OUR OWN MULTITUDE: LOS ANGELES'S BLACK PANAMANIAN COMMUNITY

JENISE MILLER

On a Saturday morning in late October, public workers in downtown Los Angeles block off the stretch of Broadway from Olympic Boulevard to Hill Street. Around 10 a.m., a crowd gathers, donned in blue and red garments, shirts embroidered with *mola*, white *polleras* with bright-colored pom-poms, or Panamanian flags draped across their backs, to celebrate the annual Panamanian Independence Day Parade. Distant relatives and former neighbors spot each other and greet each other with air kisses on each cheek. The crowd travels with the parade down Broadway and ends with a battle of Panamanian bands at Pershing Square. By activating spaces like downtown, a small but significant, interconnected community of Black Panamanians made Los Angeles their home.

While some have lived in Los Angeles since the 1960s, many Black Panamanian families moved to LA from Panama and other states such as New York, to live alongside African Americans with roots in the American South during the 1970s and 1980s. As they sought housing in areas where other Black Panamanians already lived, a constellation of Black Panamanian families and individuals grew in South Los Angeles, North Long Beach, Watts, and Compton. Decades before they migrated to the United States, their grandparents left countries like Barbados, Jamaica, Guadeloupe, Martinique, and other Caribbean islands for Panama. Like them, they relied on family, friendship, and cultural practices.

Settling into their new city, they moved to affordable homes and several apartment complexes in Compton, including an apartment complex my mother, a canteen cashier at an aerospace company, managed. Known as "The Blvd," because of its location on Long Beach Boulevard, one of Compton's major thoroughfares, Black Panamanians came to occupy over half the units in the complex. Its layout—apartments facing each other with a communal space in the front and a walkway in the back that led to the next building—encouraged neighbors to interact and kids to play together. On Saturday mornings, music poured from every apartment: Anita Baker, Johnnie Taylor, Rubén Blades, or Tabou Combo. The aroma of fried, sweet *platanos* and collard greens drifted between the apartments. During the summer, one neighbor sold *duros*, juices frozen in plastic cups, with flavors like *tamarindo*, ginger-infused jamaica, and, my favorite, *coco*, made with fresh coconut milk and shredded coconut, sweetened with cinnamon and nutmeg. If someone had a party, we all partied and feasted on delicacies such as *saus* (pickled pig feet with onions, cucumber, and white vinegar), *chicheme* (a drink made with sweetened milk, corn, and cinnamon), and Panamanian tamales (a spicy, reddish masa filled with green peas, peppers, a bone-in piece of chicken, and a prune, tripled wrapped, first in a banana leaf, then wax paper, then aluminum foil). For *Nochebuena*, my mother made pineapple glazed ham for everyone and rang in *Navidad* with the songs of Ismael Rivera, Oscar D'León, and Rubén Blades. Though the apartment's location placed us in the crosshairs of both gang violence and pedestrian-involved car accidents, we created spaces of joy by sharing Black Panamanian and African American culture and resources.

On weekends, the Black Panamanian community throughout Los Angeles came together. The physical and social proximity of Compton, Watts, North Long Beach, and South Los Angeles made it easy to gather in one another's homes or in local, public spaces. On Saturday afternoons, a group of women, which included my mother, gallivanted to local or crosstown casinos, Compton's Ramada Inn or Inglewood's Hollywood Park and Casino, to play bingo. On Sundays, they headed east, out of Los Angeles County, to San Bernardino's San Manuel Casino. If they didn't want to drive, they got together in someone's home, but kept the stakes high and brought their *plata*. The men played straight dominos in the dining room or backyard or joined the women in the living room, where you could hit on two or three in a row, before winning with the traditional five in a row. Their children commandeered the kids' room to play video games or listen to hip-hop and dancehall music, growing hungrier as time passed before the evening's host finished cooking rice and peas (red beans), *guandú* (also called *gandules* or gungo peas) or lentils, fried, sweet *platanos*, stewed chicken, and salad—potato or coleslaw. At times, food inspired the gathering, and someone prepared and sold dinners or *fritura*, fried finger foods such as *hojaldas* (a fried bread, also known as *hojaldres/dras*), empanadas, fried yucca, *patacones* (twice-fried green plantains), or *carimañolas* (mashed yucca filled with ground meat then fried). Whatever the occasion, we all ate and ate together.

Some Saturdays I accompanied my father to Victor's Upholstery Shop (known to everyone simply as Victor's shop); this meant peeking into the shop to say hello, then sitting in the car for what felt like hours while my father hung out. Initially located on Washington Boulevard in LA's Arlington Heights, the upholstery shop occupied the corner unit of a large, white brick building with peeling paint, no windows, and one front metal gate. Named for its proprietor—a slim, brown Panamanian, with a gold tooth and a Caribbean accent (like many Black Panamanians), who often dressed in a natty fit and cap—Victor opened the shop in 1965 and offered his business to the local Panamanian community. For decades, the shop doubled as a communication hub and hangout spot. If you wanted to confirm information about an event, you called Victor's shop. If you needed to purchase presale tickets for the upcoming boat cruise or dance, you could buy them at Victor's shop. When the Panamanian dictator Manuel Noriega was ousted in 1989, the local news stations came to Victor's shop to interview the Panamanian community. The layout of the space itself reflected its many functions. Bolts of fabric lined up like wallpaper on one wall, shelves with binders upon binders of swatches stacked on another wall, and a wide, wooden worktable occupied the center; it sat atop a carpet of wood dust. A dim corner room, across from the worktable and behind Victor's desk, housed a large TV and chairs. The walls were plastered with posters of athletes and bikini-clad women selling alcohol. While the sounds of Victor pounding sofa upsides with a mallet echoed through the shop, the TV room rang with the raucous laughter of men who planted themselves to talk politics and *bochinche* (gossip) in a mix of Spanish, English, and patois, drink rum and milk or

Cerveza Panama, and watch boxing matches, especially ones that featured Panama's pride, Roberto "Manos de Piedra" Duran. In exchange, they helped Victor make deliveries. As they aged, they gathered for potlucks and quieter moments.

Across from Victor's shop was Jucy's Jamaican restaurant, one of LA's few sit-down Caribbean restaurants, which has operated for more than thirty-five years. It serves similar Panamanian cuisine like chicken soup with dumplings, stewed meat dishes, and curry chicken. Sometimes we drove down Crenshaw to indulge in a beef patty from Stone Market. Opened in the 1970s, we first frequented Stone Market because it carried typical food items and brands that local stores did not, such as *guandú* peas, Malta Hatuey (a sweet, carbonated beverage), and *bacalao* (salted codfish). Outside, men sat on folding chairs or milk crates, talking and playing dancehall and old school reggae mixes that you could purchase. Over time, it became a staple in the Black Panamanian community. Located next to the market is the star of the operation: a take-out, cash only food kiosk, where dinners, patties, and the best carrot juice I've ever tasted, are prepared and sold. It is a small structure, with just a kitchen and front counter, a floor fan circulating heat and noise, and a dry-erase board that displays the menu of the day. Upon entering, the smell of coconut, butter, and cinnamon from the loaves of Coco bread and buns welcomed you the way the cashier will not. What was written on the board is what they had in stock; if an item was marked out or erased, they ran out of it for the day. If it wasn't on the board, one shouldn't ask for it (these were the unspoken rules). When an *abuelita* or other keepers of the homemade bun recipe went on a cooking hiatus, families settled for purchasing buns for Easter or Christmas from Stone Market.

During summer holidays like the Fourth of July, we celebrated at Scherer Park in Long Beach. Nicknamed "Parque Del Amo," for its location off Del Amo, between Long Beach Boulevard and Atlantic Avenue, some families arrived as early as six in the morning to claim one of the limited numbers of picnic tables, while others brought folding tables, lawn chairs, or blankets. Each family prepared meals at home and brought them to the park: coleslaw, potato salad, rice and peas or *guandú*, baked barbecue chicken, and even hot dogs and hamburgers. Occasionally, my father set up a fryer and sold *patacones* and codfish cakes. Children would go from table to table to meet up with friends. Asking for or accepting a plate from a table other than your own was a faux pas; my mother insisted that doing so constituted begging and set the trap for a good piece of *bochinche*. Folks might say that your mother did not care for you properly. The Scherer Park gatherings grew in size; at one point, someone hired an official DJ and a Panamanian ballet folklórico group performed on a portable dance floor. As Panamanians began to move to cities within San Bernardino County, festivities like an annual end of the summer picnic were held east of Los Angeles at Frank Bonelli Park in San Dimas.

Parties worthy of a formal venue took place at Shatto Banquet Hall, a rental hall on Slauson Avenue, which was popular among LA's Louisiana Creole community. We had our own version of formal wear. For men, it consisted of a button-down shirt, silk slacks, and dress shoes with no socks. Women wore glittered or sequined body-hugging dresses, extra-high heels, and a slather of gold—gold bracelets, anklets, earrings, and necklaces with *placas* (name plates or plates in the shape of the Panama Isthmus) or an *Ojo de Venado* (a round ball/amulet wrapped in gold letters). No matter the type of jewelry, it had to be gold, as the women deemed anything else *chichipatti* (cheap). At Shatto Hall, I witnessed my first and only *quinceñera*, another second-generation Black Panamanian girl, who body-rolled down the two lines of Black *damas* and *chambelanes* to Raven-Symoné's rap song "That's What Little Girls Are Made Of."

The predominant narrative about the Black Latinx community in LA claims that we suffer from isolation and are disconnected. However, it is clear that a network of Black Panamanians nurtured and created a strong sense of identity for the next generation, including myself. As a Black Panamanian in Los Angeles, I was not an anomaly. Instead, I was part of a community that held and named me.

Yet as the places and spaces known to the community changed, so did the community. Panamanians no longer live on "The Blvd." Encounters with violence and the lack of opportunity, due to divestment and the loss of jobs once provided by large industries, pushed African American and Black Panamanian families out of Los Angeles. Many followed the out-migration of African Americans east to cities like Rialto, Upland, Fontana, and Rancho Cucamonga. Folks no longer gather at Scherer Park. After decades of running his upholstery business out of Washington Boulevard, Victor had to move. This was likely a result of rising commercial rent costs and gentrification. The original location of Victor's shop is now an art gallery. He retired soon after his shop relocated. Jucy's has managed to weather the changes, while, as of 2023, Stone Market has closed.

While many families moved out of LA County, some families, including my own, remained. We moved from Compton to Long Beach, and finally, to Watts. My family arrived at these places without the community that once enriched us and made these places home. I long for that community—my mother does, too. Now, as a mother, I desire for my children to experience the affirmation that I did growing up in a Black Panamanian Los Angeles. Yet in the face of change, we remain resourceful and look to the past for guidance. As the child of migrants, I am able to do things that my parents were not able to: I can take my children to Panama. I can take them to the annual parade, the place where we still gather, and introduce them to our neighbors from "The Blvd" and our friends like Victor. Those of us who grew up nurtured by this community of Black Panamanians, and those who are just discovering it, know that in any place we gather, we are our own multitude.

BEHOLD, BUDDHA

CASSANDRA LANE

In late 2007, with our heads filled with scenes from our favorite HGTV shows, my husband and I became first-time house hunters in Los Angeles. We were short on cash and helium-high on hope.

Weighed down by student debt, we strapped our baby to my chest or his, and explored quaint bungalows in Pasadena and Altadena. Spanish-style stuccos in Leimert Park.

Four or five or six months later, our hope was a deflated balloon trapped in the wires of a telephone pole. Everything we viewed—every inhabitable thing—was out of reach. We retreated to our apartment in West Adams. Attempted to erase the images of houses that felt like ours.

Two years later, at the height of the global financial crisis, our misfortune reversed: I landed a new job as a college prep counselor for Black and Brown students at a nonprofit headquartered in Cerritos, a suburb of Los Angeles—a job paying ten grand more than my teaching job at a small high school in the Crenshaw District. Marcus and I left our apartment in the West Adams neighborhood of LA and rented a house near my new job. We spent two years reducing our debt-to-income ratio and, in 2012, made an offer on a short sale in North Long Beach that had a $250,000 sticker price.

"Oooo, be careful," my boss warned. "North Long Beach is rough around the edges."

I bristled. I have always lived on the wrong side of the tracks—or bayou, or interstate, or street. And she was not paying me enough to buy a house in a neighborhood that would warrant her approval. We are both Louisiana natives, but she, two decades my senior, grew up as part of the Black bourgeoisie. I grew up poor. Rough around the edges.

* * *

The house we bought bore no resemblance to the charming abodes of my and Marcus's fantasies. It was squat and generic, the color of spearmint gum: chewed, spit out, and smashed into the ground. Inside, a couple of holes big enough for possums to climb in and out of glared from the walls. The backyard was a hay-colored wasteland where a one-story-high brick firepit, ash-caked and forlorn, jutted out from its center.

Marcus, a newly licensed real estate agent, was representing us. He waxed on and on about the house's potential, its bones. He, who once was homeless and struggling with addiction, is always the full glass to my empty one. Pessimism is a luxury he cannot afford. His giddy visions began to pull me in; we bid and closed on the house within forty-five days (a miracle for a short sale). We spent months working with handymen—filling in holes and refurbishing wood floors, patching up plumbing and roofing problems. More months and then a year, two years, helped us warm up the rooms in earth tones, clean out and get acclimated to the ancient pit, discover backyard Persian lemon and pomegranate bushels we'd overlooked, make friends out of neighbors, and watch our kids bump up against each other's budding social skills.

Until—in 2013—I was offered a job back in the city, a position in downtown LA offering a twenty-grand hike in pay. I took it.

But I was not cut out for hour-long commuting. I told Marcus about all the new apartment buildings and restaurants I was seeing in the city center: the "new DTLA." How vibrant and alive (gentrified) the new downtown had become! And there were even families with small children and dogs. A new elementary school for downtown children was opening in the fall. If we acted fast, I said, we could try to snag a seat for our son, who would be going into the first grade.

Marcus admitted he was sick of his daily commute to and from work in Hollywood—and he missed LA. Shocking our neighbors, we left as quickly as we'd swept in. We found a lovely family to lease out our house while we rented an apartment downtown. The rent was a grand more than our mortgage, but we consoled ourselves: it was a temporary move. We watched the housing economy and paid down some more debt. In the spring of 2015, we dove into house hunting again.

This time, our budget was $400,000, pending the sale of our Long Beach house, which meant again disappointing our neighbors—and our new tenants, who'd quickly made friends with them.

We searched for months, dismayed that housing prices were once more largely out of reach. Does anything bounce back like capitalism?

One summer afternoon we were driving down Slauson Avenue, making a beeline for the creamy smoothies at Simply Wholesome, that icon that sits on the southwest corner of Overhill Drive and Slauson Avenue in an area some residents refer to as "Black Beverly Hills." We were ten blocks from Simply Wholesome when I asked Marcus to turn down a southside street cutting across Slauson to look for open house signs. I knew the dreamy houses on the northside—the hilly Black Beverly Hills side—were astronomically out of reach, but the streets on the southside of Slauson and east of Keniston Avenue are lined with modest houses filled mostly with working-class residents. As Marcus drove, I spotted a small "For Sale" sign in front of a 1920s salmon-colored stucco bungalow. I hated the color, but the house was quaint with an A-shaped façade like the houses we drew as kids. The postcard lawn was lush-green; California native plants lined the pebbled stoop.

Marcus turned off the engine.

"Oh no, not another house tour!" our son, then eight, groaned from the backseat.

"We'll just run through real quick if it's open, Sweetie," I said.

Marcus searched the address on his real estate listing database. "It's not on here."

We climbed out of the car and knocked on the door. The owner let us in to tour the house, backyard, and detached garage, which had been converted into an apartment with a full kitchen and bathroom. The main house was tiny, barely 750 square feet, but I was mesmerized by the 500-square-foot apartment. "My writing studio!" I squealed. I pulled Marcus aside. "Babe, I want it."

"I don't know, Babe," he said, shaking his head. "This house is even smaller than what we're used to."

I tried on his usual persuasive optimism. "But look at the yard. Over time, we could add onto the house. There's so much potential."

Marcus asked the owner why the house wasn't showing on the real estate database.

"Because this area is changing so much," she said. "The investors are getting older folks to sell their homes and then remodeling 'em real quick and flipping 'em for double."

"You could make a lot of money," Marcus said.

"I'm not trying to gentrify this neighborhood." She was about my mother's age. "If I can't sell to somebody Black, I'm not in a hurry to move."

Her plan was to retire in a condo in Long Beach, a place where she wouldn't have to care for a yard. I looked out the window at her yard and envisioned our son playing ball, slinging Frisbees, hosting friends. "This is it...this is the one," I told Marcus as we drove away. "This is our house."

* * *

The quasi-governmental organization I worked for was headquartered in a high-rise in downtown LA. My colleagues and I could look out the window and see the Ritz Carlton glinting gold and silver under the sun. We could glance down at the streets, where the towers cast their shadows, and see homeless men and women, walking, sleeping. At lunchtime, we cut through an alley on our way to try out one hot DTLA spot after another. Scents of baking bread and urine filled our nostrils. Middle-class and ambitious, we were sandwiched between these extremes. Closer to the ones in the shadows.

Inside the suite, the communications and public relations workstations were laid out next to each other in cubicles that reminded me of my old newspaper newsrooms. As senior writer, I helped craft and spread the organization's mission: all children, regardless of their family's economic status or zip code, deserve access to high-quality early education.

Most of my colleagues were in their early thirties to early forties. I was on the older end. When I told them that I was buying another house, their eyes lit up with curiosity. Their *OMG, congratulations!* was followed immediately by *Where?* In their eyes,

I watched numbers being crunched: my likely salary, my likely housing budget, the likeliest corners of the city I could afford. And I saw the deeper desire underneath their questions: maybe I, too, can buy a house in this city that feels so out of reach.

I answered them vaguely. "It's about ten minutes east of Culver City, adjacent to View Park, Ladera Heights, and Baldwin Hills." I dangled the jewels that hang over South Central like chandeliers.

A few days later, Amir, a Black coworker whose father is a longtime building contractor in South Central, pulled the veil off my vagueness. He was like one of my younger brothers, always roasting, always seeking to bring me down a notch. As he walked toward our work section late that morning, he yelled from across the room: "Hey guys, Cassandra ain't in no Baldwin Hills. She in the Crenshaw District. Her new house is right around the corner from Buddha's Liquor."

"Shut up, Ass," I shouted back at him. Laughing. Embarrassed. Seething.

Building inspection isn't the only inspection you undergo when buying a house.

"I never said I was in Baldwin Hills. I said I was adjacent. And I do not live around the corner from Buddha's Liquor."

"Oh, you in the hood-hood," Humberto, his PR teammate, teased.

"No, it's not the hood-hood," I snapped back.

After work, I drove to my new neighborhood and got out to walk. Our house-to-be sat in a sort of in-between, even on the same street, never mind crossing Slauson. One block west, the street begins to slope upward into an area rebranded as View Heights. The houses along that part of the street are more expansive, the sidewalks and asphalt smoother, the trees, including a family of paperbark trees, far more majestic. Keep walking and you're privy to some of the best views of the city. In 2006, screenwriter Josslyn Luckett wrote in the *Los Angeles Times* that View Heights is the "less bling" sister of Ladera Heights and those other giants. Her friend's realtor called it "the best-kept secret in all of Los Angeles."

This best-kept secret is a stone's throw from my block. Yes, someone with a good arm could stand at the end of my block, throw a stone, and hit the block that becomes View Heights. By city map-drawing, our house is part of Hyde Park, one of the oldest neighborhoods in the city. An area that, during the height of LA's gang wars, was Rollin' 60s' territory. On the northwest corner of our street, just before you cross into View Heights, lives an Old G Crip, whose front yard is a stomping ground for his fellow aging gangstas. "Oh no," I moaned to Marcus once we were in escrow. "How did we not see them in all the times we came to look at the house?"

"The owner's agent paid 'em to stay outta sight," he said, always with a joke at the ready. Deep down, he was a bit worried. He is the father of Black sons, including two adult sons from his first marriage. When we did move in, the sight of the men drinking and smoking daily, peering into cars that pass by, triggered memories he'd long ago tried to erase, except when sounding them as warning bells to his sons: you don't want that life.

He has told them about his years growing up in South Central during the crack crisis and his own stint in a gang, including how, as part of his initiation, he'd aimed a gun at a man when he was thirteen years old. He doesn't remember if the gun trembled in his hands that day, but he remembers the weight of it; he remembers watching the spark of fear shift in the man's eyes when he recognized the absolute terror in Marcus's eyes. The man had stared at Marcus a beat longer, then turned, and walked away.

South Central. Marcus got lost here—and found again.

* * *

In all my excitement over the house, I had not noticed Buddha liquor store, but as I walked east of the house and turned left at the first corner, my eyes were opened.

It was right there:

Buddha LIQUOR & MARKET.

It sits on the corner of Slauson Avenue and Rimpau Boulevard, its façade the color of melted orange sherbet, the word Buddha sitting high in white-and-red letters—a fat capital B followed by lower-case letters that lilt upward slightly, while LIQUOR & MARKET stand at attention just below it in primary blue capital letters. The sun has nearly faded one of the large posters plastered on the building ("Checks Cashed Cambio Cheques 1%"). A marquee announcing LIQUOR sticks out from the building to catch the eyes of those approaching from the side.

The store is an eyesore. How had I missed it before?

I watched Buddha in the fading light, and it became a symbol of all that is wrong in our so-called hoods across the country, where liquor stores proliferate corners, outnumbering even churches and certainly quality grocery stores and schools. Who in the world would name a liquor store after Buddha, the awakened one? Buddha advised against consuming drinks that cloud the mind and lead to heedlessness.

A man who appeared to be homeless was sleeping in a wheelchair on the sidewalk, his head hanging to one side, his neck made of rubber. Bamboozled by the promises of this Buddha's booze.

* * *

After closing escrow and renting the house back to the previous owner for a few months, we moved into our home in October 2015. As we decorated and sketched out plans to expand, it became easy to ignore Buddha. For my morning and evening walks,

I chose the prettier streets, steered clear of Slauson. When driving, it was easy enough to circumvent that intersection—and the Old G corner.

A friend came over one night to see the house. I beamed under her compliments about the décor. Her family was outgrowing their apartment, and I imagined them finding a house around the corner, our kids growing up together and us figuring out how to navigate the complicated road of educating our children in the city. Together. Before crossing the threshold to leave, she turned back to me and grabbed my hand. "Sand, is it safe here? Do you feel safe?"

I crossed my arms over my chest. Her eyes followed my movements before finding my eyes again. "I feel safe," I said, coughing up a laugh. Her question dredged up a small, gnawing fear I harbored that some friends might not feel comfortable visiting us here—and it dredged up old sensations of shame about lack.

"I looked up crime stats before we made our offer and things have been calm around here for a while."

Things are certainly not all the way calm. But I felt defensive and protective of the neighborhood's image. I was part and parcel of it now and, in a way, always have been.

✳ ✳ ✳

My home state, Louisiana, holds up the rest of the country on one tattered, boot-clad foot. It is both everything outsiders imagine it to be and everything their imaginations could never plumb. A red state, yes, but also Black. One of the poorest states in the union, but also one of the richest—precisely because of its Black gold.

When I was growing up, most of the Black folks in my hometown lived in Old Heights—a tract of modest and dilapidated houses woven together on streets named after trees. The house I grew up in was on Elm Street, and it was one of the dilapidated ones. There are layers of haves and have-nots radiating within the collectively disenfranchised. My multigenerational family lived in a house that, as a child, I was ego-crushingly embarrassed of because it had a mind of its own: the back end of the house sunk down like a dejected dog's limp tail.

On the way home from school, I watched the neighborhoods outside the bus window go from desirable to wanting, but I loved the ribbon of train tracks that cut across Old Heights. The rocks lining the tracks looked like a never-ending river of diamonds—a million shining bodies creating an equator between Us and Them. I liked to collect a couple of rocks every now and then, nestling the jagged and hot stones in my pockets.

There was something comforting about growing up in a Black neighborhood; there was no one there to make us feel as though we didn't belong. Grandmama's friends looked out for us; the Tamale Man nourished us; Miss Fannie Mae's frozen cups and sugar cookies spoiled us.

As an adult, my inner compass magnetizes me to neighborhoods that remind me of home.

✳ ✳ ✳

In the late 1990s, my first husband, Ric, and I lived in New Orleans's Mid-City. Our double shotgun house sat on the side of Bayou St. John, which was mostly made up of working-class Black residents. On the other side of the bayou stood houses occupied by more affluent residents, mostly white. One night, we attended a colleague's house party on that side. We were talking to a group of white reporters when one of them asked, "Where do guys stay?"

"Right here by the bayou," I said. "We walked here."

"Oh wow," she said. "What side are you on?"

My eyes narrowed. The Black side. "The French Quarter side," I said.

"Oh," she said, the vowel popping out of her mouth, high-pitched and quick.

“Damn, I should’ve said it,” I told Ric on our walk back to our place. He’d grown up in ’70s Harlem. He’d polished his rough edges to a high sheen. Just underneath the veneer, though, lay something sharp, jagged, beautiful. We laughed, imagining the shock on the woman’s face if I’d said what had wanted to be said.

Restraint is not all it’s cracked up to be. Letting your rough edges rip every now and then is cathartic.

There was a time I thought I’d die and be buried in New Orleans, but Ric didn’t love it enough to stay forever. He is a photojournalist, an explorer, a pioneer. Eventually I, too, heard the call toward something more expansive. The West.

We left New Orleans—that wet and fecund place—for greener pastures. In the desert. For all its dryness, it has been fertile for me. After our divorce, Ric left to explore lands beyond this country’s borders, but I have stayed, steadfast despite all my changing of jobs and place and partner. And twenty years in, I am still getting to know this city that everyone loves to stereotype. “I don’t think stereotypes are problematic because they’re false,” Chimamanda Ngozi Adichie says. “I think they are problematic because they’re incomplete.”

Stereotypes about South Central as a whole, or about the streets on the south side of Slauson, or the streets east of Keniston are incomplete. My image of Buddha Liquor & Market is incomplete.

It took me about a year to finally step inside the store. A Santa Clarita man, Elias Aramouni had recently bought the store from a woman named Annie Shin who had, in 2013, made the papers. She was being boycotted by some Black residents because of a rumor that she was really Soon Ja Du, the woman who shot and killed fifteen-year-old Latasha Harlins while Latasha was trying to buy orange juice from Du’s Liquor Store in 1991.

Years can pass, decades, and something masquerading as progress can waltz in, rebranding South Central as South LA, doubling housing prices, shifting the racial and economic makeup of a neighborhood once seen as all kinds of wrong, but roots of resentment, anxiety, and distrust run deep.

As do the memories that bring us profound joy. Which is what a part of me feels now when I walk inside Buddha, where Aramouni has remodeled the interior, and see Louisiana food stuffs—boudin, Camellia red beans, andouille sausage—that are hard to come by in a place so far away from home. I delight, too, in grabbing candies I used to cherish as a child at the corner store in my Louisiana neighborhood: Red Hots, Lemonheads, banana-flavored Now and Laters. Out of all the LA neighborhoods I’ve lived in, this is the one that feels most like home, this place where Blacks migrating from Louisiana during the Great Migration were able to settle when a supposedly less racist Los Angeles barred them from other neighborhoods.

Just up the street from Buddha, in Black Beverly Hills, sits what I call "Little Louisiana," where my family and I get po'boys and pralines from Orleans and York, New Orleans snoballs from SnoBall Shop, gumbo and Zydeco music at La Louisanne, founded in the 1960s by Ed Wheeler, who left our home state in 1962 and never returned.

When I want to return to my roots in my own kitchen, using my own hands, a stop at Buddha is a must.

"The other day, I asked the owner when he was going to fix up the outside," Marcus said recently after I brought back boudin and andouille from Buddha on Mardi Gras, which we planned to celebrate in the home we've now expanded, or in the backyard Marcus transformed into our own little "Shangri-la" during the first year of the pandemic.

I put my bags down on the table and laughed. "I spoke to the owner today and asked him the same thing."

Through changing owners, through uprisings, through the murder and mourning of Nipsey Hussle just a few blocks away, Buddha has been a steadfast fixture.

"There are so many of you Louisianians in this area, and lots of them who've moved far away to places like Lancaster, Palmdale," Aramouni told me. But they come all the way here for boudin and other stuff we have they can't find anywhere else." He tried to change the store's name when he first bought it, but it caused an uproar. "I made a huge mistake," he says. "I had to get a DBA [Doing Business As] to operate as Buddha Market. The name means a lot to people. People who tell me they remember coming here with their mothers and grandmothers back in the '50s and '60s." The previous owners left their small jade statue of the laughing Buddha, and Aramouni keeps it on top of a soda refrigerator. Sticky dust clings to the laughing Buddha's bald head, shoulders, and belly.

In this rapidly changing neighborhood, the house we bought for $400,000 is, just seven years later, valued at more than double that amount. "What a gem this neighborhood is," a real estate agent showing a house for $900,000 just around the corner told me a couple of years ago. "Slauson is so misleading." And yet, our new, upwardly mobile neighbors are dismayed at the police helicopters that circle, the fireworks that last for months after July 4 or the new year, the lack of a quality grocery store in the immediate vicinity, the pockets of blight they overlooked in their eagerness to move into investors' remodeled homes that remind them of the homes they couldn't afford in Culver City, West LA, or Larchmont.

"It's like the neighborhood hasn't caught up to their million-dollar investments yet," my neighborhood Zumba friend Megan says.

The only thing standing between my house and Slauson is an alley, and on the other side of that alley are the storefronts—many of them boarded up and graffitied—that stand across from Buddha Market. Lately, I've been obsessed with an idea of opening up a bread bakery in one of them, of joining forces with the entrepreneurs and visionaries whose new businesses and projects inspire me. There would be a garden and patio and a community program to help feed those who don't own a home on either side of Slauson or anywhere else. Maybe, I think, our little pocket of beauty could inspire Aramouni to fix up Buddha. He tells us that he ran out of money before he could renovate the store's exterior, that he has plans to clean up the outside.

We will keep pressing. Backed up by a double train of sky-high palms that South Central is famous for, Buddha could be a thing of beauty. On my walks, I watch it in different lights and from different angles.

And Buddha watches me.

IN THE RUBBLE: PICTURING LA'S HOUSING CRISIS

DAVID HELPS

No one knew how long the house at 11560 Link St. had been abandoned, but the neighbors wanted it gone. On a February morning in 1990, Tom Bradley, Los Angeles's first Black mayor, stood in front of the graffitied and crumbling bungalow in the Harbor Gateway neighborhood. Here in South LA, where neighbors endured both the crack cocaine trade and the militarized police response, dilapidated "rock houses" became a lightning rod. Addressing the assembled group of journalists, Bradley congratulated his administration for its war on these "neighborhood nightmares."[1] On the mayor's signal, a bulldozer roared into motion and reduced the structure to a heap of wood, concrete rubble, and broken glass. Today, there is no "11560" Link Street. It's been overwritten—a smaller house with a new number stands in its place.

By the late 1980s, years of austerity and job loss had taken their toll on South Los Angeles neighborhoods. Perhaps no part of the built environment symbolized urban decline better than blighted homes: reminders of the middle class that left and the resources they took with them. The Link Street property, however, was not simply vacant. When the City's Bureau of Community Safety dispatched someone to photograph the site in 1989, they found only a burned-out shell. What is striking about the pictures is not only the extent of the damage, but that a routine code inspection would generate such aestheticized images. In saturated black and white, the Southern California sun is unforgiving. Mike Davis famously wrote in his 1990 book *City of Quartz* that Los Angeles is only ever depicted one of two ways: as sunshine or as noir. The Link Street photographs are striking because they reveal the one within the other, urban danger drenched in sunlight.

Despite their artistic allure, the photographs served a purely documentary purpose. They came to me as crime scene evidence, so to speak. Once developed, the Link Street photographs found their way to the desk of Tom Bradley, and eventually into his mayoral papers after he left office three years later. Today, they're tucked inside a folder labeled "Operation Knockdown 1990."[2]

A few weeks before the Link Street demolition, Mayor Bradley had announced that the built environment would be the new front in the City's war on drugs. Dubbed "Operation Knockdown," the program enlisted the Los Angeles Police Department to identify drug trafficking sites for demolition. In the span of one year, LA bulldozed at least 215 alleged "crack houses."[3] In February 1990, the bungalow on Link Street joined them in the rubble.

The bulldozer shaped the life of twentieth-century cities more than almost any other innovation. Between 1949 and 1974, the federal government poured more than six billion dollars into "urban renewal" in cities and inner ring suburbs. Urban renewal promised to stimulate private investment, improve the nation's housing stock, and demonstrate American Cold War superiority by lifting hundreds of thousands of families out of poverty. The 1949 Housing Act committed the government to building 810,000 new housing units by 1955. But white opposition to racial integration and to public housing made razing slums easier than building livable homes to replace them. Renters made up the majority of the displaced, with Black and Latinx residents significantly overrepresented. LA's largest urban renewal project—the demolition of Bunker Hill—displaced almost three thousand households, according to the researchers behind the *Mapping Inequality* public history project.

The 1980s gave blight removal a perverse law-and-order twist. This was the height of the crack abuse epidemic, and everywhere the metaphors of "total war" were swirling. Police and prosecutors constantly described their task as a Vietnam-like war of attrition. Speaking to a reporter for *Newsweek* in 1985, a Black woman from the South Central Organizing Committee compared her own block to Lebanon, whose civil war had just introduced "suicide bombing" into the global vernacular. If the fight against drugs and gangs was indeed a war, Operation Knockdown made sure that it would be fought over scorched earth.

The bungalow at 11560 Link St. held a unique distinction among Operation Knockdown targets. It was the first structure destroyed after the Los Angeles City Council hurriedly passed a sixty-day moratorium on demolitions in late January 1990. The moratorium came just days after the *Los Angeles Times* revealed that some of the demolished buildings were either occupied, had no connection to the drug trade, or might have been repaired.

Thirty-three-year-old Henry Smith told the reporter how he watched the destruction of his childhood home, which belonged to a family member living out of state, just two days after Christmas. "I've lived here since elementary school," he protested. "I'll have to move to Skid Row after they tear it down."[4]

With this exposé, the *Los Angeles Times* told a story about good intentions. In its urgent war on drugs, the logic went, the City failed to consider the collateral damage. This was beside the point, since Mayor Bradley publicly admitted that the Bureau of Community Safety never defined what counted as an unrepairable structure—let alone demonstrated that any of the targets were sites of illegal activity. Only after the exposé did the City establish a protocol to inform owners about City loans that they could apply for to bring their building up to code. Operation Knockdown continued, even with the moratorium in effect, as the city council approved the demolition of structures like 11560 Link St.

Whatever the City's intentions, one consequence was clear. Operation Knockdown reduced the already scarce supply of affordable housing at the very moment that homelessness became a mass phenomenon, and one experienced overwhelmingly by Black and Brown Angelenos suffering the brunt of deindustrialization and cuts to public health programs like drug counseling.

Given the new scrutiny on Operation Knockdown, the Bureau of Community Safety did its research on 11560 Link St. According to the agency's files, police first reported the building in August 1988, and an inspection later that month found it to be vacant.[5] And though it lacked the Hollywood features of a drug hideout—steel door, guard dogs, Uzi-toting gangsters—the inspection photographs make clear the impossibility of a simple rehab.

It was a different kind of crime scene. Many of Operation Knockdown's targets, including the Link Street bungalow, began their rapid deterioration as foreclosures. Beginning in 1980, Washington passed legislation that incentivized risky real estate lending, expanded the secondary mortgage market, removed strict conflict of interest rules, and significantly lowered the amount of capital that banks needed to have on hand to be considered solvent. In California especially, predatory lending, a burst housing bubble, and outright fraud within the mortgage industry unleashed a deluge of foreclosures. Nationally, more than 385,000 federally insured mortgages entered into foreclosure between 1983 and 1987 alone, according to historian Dustin Walker. Communities like South LA, where redlining had long prevented residents from obtaining federally insured mortgages, became prey to newly unsupervised lenders. "Zombie institutions" like Westwood Savings and Loan and Gibraltar Savings of Beverly Hills continued to originate, buy, and sell subprime mortgages for years even after they were technically and legally bankrupt.

Among the worst offenders in the 1980s was Citicorp Mortgage, which grew its market share exponentially by paying kickbacks to realtors who aggressively steered their clients toward Citicorp loans. Among Citicorp's foreclosures in this period: 11560 Link St.

The magical thinking that allows mortgages to be packaged and traded, manipulated in value, and collectively insured by federal regulators, for more money than the agencies even have on hand, must eventually touch down somewhere. Time and again, that wreckage has occurred in under-resourced and hyper-exploited communities like South LA. Predatory mortgage lenders inflated the housing bubble until it popped, transforming Black and Brown people's homes into foreclosures. The transformation of a house into rubble—the pulverization of concrete and glass and metal—releases potentially lead- and asbestos-laden dust into the environment.

In this life cycle of creative destruction, Angelenos of color suffered at every stage. In 1994, when the Northridge earthquake destroyed parts of the Santa Monica Freeway, a concrete recycling company dragged the rubble to Huntington Park, an industrial town in the LA Harbor region whose population is 97% Latinx. The mound of rubble measured 150 feet—residents called it "La Montaña." Residents believed the site would be used for polluted soil and debris from the construction of the Alameda Corridor, a rail line linking the LA and Long Beach ports, so the region can better compete with other hubs of global trade. Community members began to report nosebleeds and breathing problems like asthma and bronchitis. After years of activism, Huntington Park shut down the recycling facility in 2002. The effort to remove La Montaña began three years later.

To perceive something as weird is to recognize that it is out of place, like a mountain of concrete rubble in the middle of a residential neighborhood. "The weird is marked by an exorbitant presence, a teeming which exceeds our capacity to represent it," the late Mark Fisher wrote in *The Weird and the Eerie*. The eerie, by contrast, is the inescapable sensation that something is missing. The discomfort that comes with looking at the Link Street photographs is in the reminder that this rubble had been someone's home.

Finance capital continues to wreak havoc on California housing markets. Two years ago, LA banned short-term rentals for properties that are not a primary residence. The measures aimed to cut down on speculation and free up homes that are vacant most of the year. By failing to devote resources to enforce the measure, however, as many as six thousand illegal short-term rentals remained listed on Airbnb alone in 2020, a *Los Angeles Times* investigation found. According to local housing advocates, the enforcement vacuum has enabled landlords to mass-evict tenants in order to convert housing into hotel rooms in locations where zoning would otherwise prohibit running a hotel. The City's unwillingness or inability to contain these unregulated units has earned them the nickname of "home-wreckers."

More than thirty years after the demolition of 11560 Link St., people in cities across the US have issued the demand to make #BlackHomesMatter. "A home is not just bricks and mortar," the legal scholar Bernadette Atuahene reminded an audience of housing advocates and journalists in Detroit in 2021. "A home is a family's memories, a family's legacy. It's how we pass down intergenerational wealth."

Los Angeles has one of the lowest rates of homeownership in the country. The pandemic pushed thousands of renters and mortgage holders to the brink. As of fall 2020, more than ten percent of LA homeowners were behind on their mortgage while one in five renters couldn't afford their rent. With protections against evictions and foreclosures expired, as many as one million metro LA households face possible displacement, according to research by the Terner Center for Housing Innovation at UC Berkeley.

We often struggle to imagine these things as "violence" or "crimes." It's true that in the wake of the savings and loan crash, a number of fraudsters were prosecuted; a few were even convicted. But convictions—like home demolitions—bypassed solutions for the real victims. No one regained shelter, or intergenerational wealth, or a family's memories just because a crooked banker went to prison. The images of 11560 Link St. are crime scene photos only once you know what's outside the frame.

Confronting the housing crisis requires new ways of seeing. It means heeding the words of the abolitionist scholar and filmmaker Brett Story in her book *Prison Land*: "Let us look everywhere, so that we can act anywhere."

CORNTASSEL

CAROLYN M. DUNN

One of my passions that I have gotten away from these last few years is my garden. Though the front yard looks like an English cottage garden, the back has needed some help. But since my mother's passing, I finally feel like this is my house now. It was the house I grew up in, the place where my roots are, but for the last six years, during which we moved from our house into my mom's—it never felt like mine. Moving from my own place—having been on my own and then a wife and mom—and going back to my mom's house was a harder transition than I thought it would be. We moved in with her because of her dementia, but soon after, we had to hire twenty-four-hour caregivers. Her health deteriorated so much that it became tough to manage with my work and being a parent. The caregivers became part of our family and when my mom passed away, we lost not only the shell of who she was, but we also lost the caregivers who had become so close to us. This forced us to become just us five again, and although it's been a tough transition, we have made a go of it. I have never really written of my mom's life in the last few years and how it felt to be a motherless daughter when the shell of her was still walking around in a haze of a netherworld that she seemed to hover within and without. I had grieved for her long ago.

She was a tough nut, my mom, throughout my childhood and adulthood. While we were in close contact for what would become the rest of her life, she was an emotionally distant parent. We grew close after my dad passed in 1990; losing my sister, then my father, took an emotional toll on her, and that grief was channeled into a bond we'd never before shared. My mother was raised in Los Angeles, born in the 1930s in a multicultural neighborhood in Watts long before Watts became Watts. The central organizing principle of their lives was family, and their religion. Creole Catholics from Louisiana, they were long radicalized by a religion that started out as French and became Indigenized and Africanized into something that they shaped into their own. Their family took up a city block of its own, and when my mother and her siblings—my aunt and their first cousin, who was like a brother to them their whole lives—came into adulthood with children and spouses of their own, they settled in San Pedro in the late 1960s, early 1970s. San Pedro was our base, our family compound. Like our family home in Watts, where we took up a whole city block, our little family grouping took up residence in the cliffs above the ocean where we were within shouting distance of one another.

We grew up radical social justice warriors in a working-class town that was full of immigrants who brought their ideals of the "old world" (Italy, Croatia) to the "new

IT WAS BETTER BEFORE THEY CAME

world." The erasure of the Tongva villages continued with Columbus Day parades, Knights of Columbus, and conservative Catholicism that came directly, it seemed, from Rome itself. Our family brought its own "old world" (Louisiana) sensibility to our settled homelands, but we grew up Creole–Choctaw/Biloxi, French and African and Japanese-American with my Nissei aunt whose family endured relocation from their home community in Pismo Beach to internment at Camp Topaz in Utah for almost five years. Our ocean alignments–Gulf Coast and Central California coast—met West Coast, and we wandered the spaces of Tongva ocean life, recognizing the land we had settled and the people who inhabited it still. We grew up with family stories as well as those of our settled homeland while living life on the ocean: fishing every weekend, exploring the tidepools at Royal Palms, spending time boating along and outside of the kelp beds, greeting seals and dolphin relatives. This ocean current connected us to the Gulf currents back home. This ocean home was the only one my generation knew, but our Gulf blood still flowed freely, mingling with the Pacific currents of our Tongva and Chumash relatives. It seemed only we were aware of the Tongva world around us—the people, the stories, the stars, the sky and the earth that was plentiful, because we were a part of that world. Our stories engaged with Tongva stories, and we became Indigenous diasporic settlers within another Indigenous homeland. The community welcomed and embraced us, and we embraced them.

Then it was just us and our extended family, and when my mother was diagnosed with Alzheimer's-like dementia in 1997, it was just plain unfair. But all the supercoping skills she instilled within me helped me through the most difficult times in 1997 and later, when I started graduate school with a new baby, a toddler, a kindergartner, an ailing parent, and a spouse with difficulties of his own. All of this is to say that when we moved into my mom's house, my gardening fell away. There is something genetic about agriculture; it's in the blood and I have to do it. We lived on a sloped terrace, ideal for corn, beans, squash, melons, okra, peppers, tomatoes, and other growing vines—but the lack of actual flat yard space proved difficult, so I put the family garden off.

Eventually, my husband built me three large raised beds in the backyard in preparation for our terraced garden for next year. We planted the usual corn, beans, squash, tomatoes, melons, and tobacco; these plants were indigenous transplants whose knowledge grew in our blood. Like us, they grew in soil that had been cultivated by Tongva lives and stories as well as Tongva blood. My friend Teresa, herself a diasporic Karuk Indian living in Paiute homelands, sent seeds from her family's Sun Dance garden, and the kids and I had a grand time planting. When the seedlings sprouted shortly after, I was so excited. I can see why some folks consider those plants children—to actually care and nurture and plant and make sure they grow to fruition. Now that's ceremonial performativity in action. One week we had corntassel, another week, corn silk. We went out to sing a song for our plants, for continued growth and development... for whatever might show up next.

It has been fifteen years since the garden grew, since that corntassel sprouted in a Biloxi/Choctaw/Mvskoke/Ishak garden in Southern California. The corn silk is long gone, blown away in memory and dust, like the stars we are only now seeing at the beginnings of the universe, traveling through space and time. For Indigenous peoples, we have a different relationship with space and time that the Western world tells us does not exist. Our memories exist in our worlds long after they are gone, like the stars we are only now seeing through the lens of a Western-made telescope floating just off the Earth's orbit in space. My mother joined the Ancestors in the stars, where like the stars, she has been reborn as an Ancestor who lives and breathes within the expanse of the Universe. Our home was left behind and sold, remade in the image of a different star, by one of my childhood friends. I like to think that the house is still in the family, since my childhood friend grew up there with me. Time and space coming together in San Pedro as she raised her children in the home where my children also grew, like cornstalks, toward adulthood. We share the memories of growing up there with our children, and our children will carry those memories through time and space as well.

In May of 2005, a group calling itself Save Our State attacked the Danzas Indigenous monument at the Metrorail train station in Baldwin Park, California. The monument, designed and installed by the renowned artist Judith F. Baca, became a point of controversy in which Judy Baca's life was threatened as well as the lives of the mayor and city council of Baldwin Park. When we interviewed Judy and Mayor Manuel Lozano, KPFK and American Indian Airwaves also became targets of Save Our State members and their allied groups. The monument itself is beautiful, a testament to the cultures that inhabit the basin. Especially moving is the tribute to Toypurina, the Tongva spiritual leader who led an uprising against the Spanish in California. A quote from a former Baldwin Park councilman is part of the monument: "It was better before they came." This man was white, lamenting the "arrival" of Latinos and Chicanos in the San Gabriel Valley. Ahh, St. Gabriel the Archangel. The messenger of God, the angelic mouthpiece "Who speaks for God." He from whom the Tongva inherited the name Gabrieleño, after the mission that raped and sodomized them, forced the songs from their mouths with lye and ash. Gabrieleño. Juaneno. Mission Boulevard. San Pedro. La Puebla de la Reina de Los Angeles. Our Lady, Queen of the Angels, hear this prayer. Indigenous California genocide is practiced in the words that celebrate this gloriously romantic Spanish fantasy past, the past that meant death and burnt offerings of Native flesh to appease the priests whose names are now elevated to sainthood. They became saints by killing Indians. Our best revenge is surviving them.

I have come full circle, returning to my beloved homeland of Los Angeles after many years gone—to the homelands of the Amah Mutsun, the Ojibwe of the Saginaw Chippewa Indian Tribe, and most recently to the relocated homelands of my own Creek and Cherokee relatives, where we live in the traditional homelands of the Kickapoo and Comanche. No matter where I have lived, there is always recognition of the Indigenous communities in whose space I have settled. Connections to communities as Indigenous peoples are vital for our survival as Indigenous diasporic peoples. I am fortunate to have been welcomed by Indigenous communities where my children and I have occupied. As a professor, I am always talking with my students about colonization and conquest. This is my world as a colonized person, and my work in decolonial praxis as an Indigenous person and as a relocated settler matters in these conversations. What does it mean to name a place? What are the political ramifications of the renaming, the taking away, the erasure of history, language, and place? We are reminded daily of the colonial encounter, the murders in the name of God, in the concrete channel of the Los Angeles River as the Army Corps of Engineers forced her meandering all the way to the ocean. What does she think of all of this, of the trash and cars and dirt and silt and shopping carts and bicycles and car engines and everything else put in this falsified river, this ancient place of water that still runs through angels and stars, dust and ash? Does she know the words we speak when standing on the bridge, dropping tobacco leaves and sage to her? Maybe the English, some Spanish. But can she recognize the Biloxi/Choctaw/Mvskoke/Ishak/Congolese/French song that followed my grandparents here? Does she know the spirits that accompany me, echoing my breath on the shore after the rain I sang for?

> *It was better before they came, she tells me, in a language I understand, in the world of water and life, there was no room for arrogance, for mastery. There is balance, there is hope. For thousands of years, I have run the course of this land unbound, my desires unbroken, like the sparkling stones leave for me among various places I travel. The stones whisper to me of "A good harvest this year, Payit, I pray," or "Bless my children with rain, Payit," and "May the acorns grow plentiful and unburdened, Payit," or "May I see desire reflected in his eyes only for me, I implore, Payit..." I take their words and go on my way.*
>
> *When the sparkling stones and words became few, I still heard their prayers, whispered upon a breath of smoke, a piece of grief. "May I stand the touch of the padre on my flesh, Payit, so my children won't grow hungry another night," or "May my songs be sung on the devil winds to reach the ears of the maker of breath, Payit," and "May it all be worth the death of my father, Payit, to peel the flesh from their bones in remembrance of my home," then I began to know their fear.*
>
> *I, however, did not fear. It is not within me to fear. I ran. I flowed. I called the rain and she heard me. Moving upon the landscape, we took over the shores, taking their horses, their cattle, their dogs, their farms.*
>
> *Once, I took a Spanish child who wandered too far from home. I called her Tiat. She became brown from the sun and my love. I adored her too much to release her, so I gave her back to the people so she could ferry them across*

oceans and stars to bring rain, bring seeds, bring songs to the relatives across skies. Tiat knows she is my child. There is no memory of Francisca, the name the friars gave her. She knows she is Tiat, child of Payit, the river of life, bringer of rain and songs.

It was better before they came.

The sparkling stones became no longer plentiful and the tongue of the friars became prayers of rage to my ears. They were castaways, the ones nobody wanted, so they came to me, and I sheltered them in my arms. They would know my heart, my words, and they would follow me across deepening daylight skies and hollowed dreams of night, upon the breath of the ocean and stars to where I joined them, on the shore, singing.

TO EAT A FIG IS TO SWALLOW GHOSTS

KENJI C. LIU

zuihitsu

A fig fruit is composed of hundreds, sometimes thousands of tiny flowers, florets, hidden inside a fleshy covering. This inside-out world is why we never see fig flowers.

Some might think of oranges when quizzed about Southern California fruit, but oranges originated in China.

In science fiction, a Dyson sphere is a massive shell built to completely enclose a star in order to capture its total energy output. By containing the star, the sphere completely blocks all outgoing visible light, altering the way it appears to outside observers.

This hidden, inside-out world is why we might never be able to see advanced extraterrestrial civilizations.

Without the knowledge and experience of immigrant Chinese agricultural workers, California's orange industry would have died quickly.

Los Angeles has been the site of many science fiction stories, most notably *Blade Runner*. It is notable for how thoroughly it enacts an Orientalist fantasy of a 2019 where "Asianness" has saturated society, but without any actual Asian people. We are an implied threat, but without us, there is no future.

There's an orchid (*Ophrys apifera*) that looks like a certain female bee in order to attract certain male bees. But the bee is extinct. The orchid continues to testify to a bee that no longer exists. The bee is implied.

Some fig trees require a special female wasp to pollinate their flowers and grow fruit. In return, the fig offers the wasp a place to lay its eggs and reproduce.

Spanish missionaries introduced figs to California. But the fig wasp hadn't been brought to the colonization, and the fig kept waiting for her. The Mission fig (*Ficus caricia*) was bred to produce fruit without the wasp. The wasp is missing in our *Blade Runner* future.

☀

The fig is the third tree to be mentioned in the *Bible*. Adam and Eve used its leaves to cover their nakedness after Eve supposedly messed things up for them.

☀

It's just like a colonizer to think he should cut female fig wasps out of the picture.

☀

The self-pollinating fig is the ghost of conquest. It's a memory of colonization. Does it remember the wasp? It might not; colonization is like that. But when we eat a Mission fig, we eat the fruit of conquest.

☀

In the fig community, there are different family arrangements. Some types of fig trees are monoecious, which means they grow both "male" and "female" flowers. Others are dioecious, in which some trees offer "male" and "female" flowers and other trees only have "female" flowers. All need special "female" wasps to facilitate pollination. Nature is naturally queer.

☀

There's a giant Moreton Bay fig tree (*Ficus macrophylla*) in the heart of Little Tokyo, planted around 1920 by Reverend Shutai Aoyama of the Koyasan Buddhist congregation in front of its temple many years ago. The temple has moved, but the tree remains, watching over the block.

☀

In some Buddhist traditions, contemplating the impermanence of the body is a way to develop equanimity and compassion for self and others. A person is basically a fig, thousands of flowers inside a fleshy covering, growing, opening, closing, passing away.

☀

Close the eyes, turn inward. Notice the weight of our bodies on the earth. Watch the breath enter and leave the body. Watch feelings, thoughts, and sensations flower and pass.

☀

It is hard to see what's happening inside a person, just as it is with a fig or a Dyson sphere.

☀

The Japanese word for fig tree, 無花果, is composed of the *kanji* for "no" (無)—a particle of negation—"flower" (花) and "fruit" (果). This refers to a tree that bears fruit without flowering. The ancient pictogram for 無 was a person holding something in both hands, but since then, it has come to denote not having.

☀

無 can be read as "*mu*," which means nothingness, or a response to a Zen koan that has neither a yes or no answer. Rather than divide into a binary, "*mu*" refutes the question.

The problem with a Dyson sphere is it has a huge surface area, which makes it vulnerable to comets and meteorites. A meteor impact could throw the whole thing off-center, or burst through to the interior. An alternate vision is a tight network of stations weaving around the sun.

The ancient root of the word "wasp" is possibly related to "weave." Weave can refer to interlacing a material together, but also to devising.

A strangler fig grows and envelops a host tree. Once the host tree dies and decomposes, it leaves a long hollow inside the fig tree.

Early Spanish missionary colonization established itself near Native American towns and villages, tried to envelop and strangle them.

The Aoyama fig tree is located in a parking lot; it grows straight up from asphalt and concrete. It is one of the only direct connections to the actual dirt below. It is also a strangler fig. What lives in its center? An entrance and exit for ghosts.

The fig's response: 無 (*mu*).

If the star inside a Dyson sphere was to die and vanish, what would be left?

The Buddha was enlightened after sitting in meditation under a fig tree (*Ficus religiosa*) for many days in Bodh Gaya, India. Though the original tree was destroyed and replaced, a branch from the original was rooted elsewhere, in Sri Lanka.

The problem with people is that we are vulnerable to everything. Almost anything can throw us off-center.

The Buddhist insight of *anatta*, or no-self, reminds us that although we may have an experience of the self as continuous, when you get down to it, we are constantly changing, without a solid center. Empty of a true self.

The adjective "empty" evolved from the Old English word for "leisure." The modern Greek word for "empty" evolved from a word meaning "freedom from fear."

In Shinto, giant trees are often sites for local gods. Properly imbued with sacred ropes and paper streamers, they become indistinguishable from gods.

There is an infamous black-and-white photo of the corner of First and Central, a block south of the Aoyama fig tree. It shows MPs forcing Japanese Americans onto buses headed to horse stalls at Santa Anita racetrack, then concentration camps.

Only a few more blocks away, next to the historic founding site of Los Angeles, is where an 1871 race riot took place in which dozens of Chinese people were shot and hanged by a mob of hundreds.

Los Angeles without Asians seems speculative, but they already tried to make it happen.

Gods, too, are implied by the empty spaces present in the everyday, leaving us wondering what or who could possibly have created this world.

The adjective "hollow" is said to originate in an ancient Proto-Indo-European root word, meaning "to cover, conceal, save."

A Dyson sphere would only be possible because of extremely advanced technologies, which for us would probably be indistinguishable from magic or deities.

Next to the site of the 1871 massacre of dozens of Chinese is a park dedicated to Father Junipero Serra, who oversaw the system of California missions. Under the missions, Native Americans were decimated by disease, torture, forced labor, and starvation.

☀

In the Bible, Jesus curses a fig tree for having no fruit for him. He goes on to Jerusalem where he drives out capitalists from the temple. The next day, they pass the same fig tree, which has withered. Some scholars say this symbolizes his fight against a lack of righteousness. Others say this is an example of a miracle wasted in service to a bad temper.

☀

The fig's response: 無 (*mu*).

☀

Freeman Dyson, who came up with what's now called a Dyson sphere, was a climate change skeptic who served on an advisory board for a conservative climate change think tank.

☀

Figs and wasps have been helping each other out for about 65 million years, since dinosaurs were thumping around Los Angeles.

☀

In Los Angeles 2020, Indigenous activists toppled the statue of Junipero Serra. In the social media video, someone can be heard yelling, "This is for our ancestors!"

☀

Some fig wasps live up to two months; others only live one to two days. Research indicates that an increase of three degrees in global temperatures would dramatically decrease the life span of fig wasps.

☀

Climate change skepticism rings hollow in the face of actual weather.

☀

Things a female fig wasp probably hates:

- Burrowing into a fig and finding another wasp already there.
- Male wasps not acknowledging the immense amount of labor involved in pollinating and laying eggs.
- When another wasp comes calling in the middle of the night and overstays their welcome in the morning.
- Figs who act superior because they don't need a pollinator.
- Dying inside the wrong fig.

☀

Some female figs can pretend to be male figs in order to seduce the female wasp. The wasp enters and pollinates, but cannot lay her eggs. She dies, and the fig digests her. Her ghost gives life to the fig.

☀

Wasps and trees don't actually give a fig about gender.

☀

In Los Angeles, there are a lot of fig trees, though you have to know what they look like. Usually, they aren't just out in the open, waving their figs around. But they haunt the city's corners; occasionally, you meet one.

☀

I hadn't tasted a fresh fig before moving to California. I did really like Fig Newtons.

☀

When eating a fig, we are also eating the ghost of a female wasp.

☀

If fig wasps went extinct, could the remaining fig trees testify to the memory of their insect partner?

☀

The old saying, I don't give a fig, implies that figs are of low value.

☀

The fig's response: 無 (*mu*).

LOST

DAVID L. ULIN

The streets I was walking were not unfamiliar. On the other hand, they were not familiar enough. I was in South Robertson—or as the city calls it, Reynier Village, although I had never heard the term before. My wife and I were staying in an Airbnb on Olin Street, just north of Hamilton High School. We had once tried to buy a house around the corner, on Hargis Street, across from Reynier Park. We'd been outbid; we were always outbid. This is one reason we remain renters now. The house had a koi pond in a small backyard; we dreamt of sitting beside it as our children played with the kids from Shenandoah Street Elementary School. My wife had never quite gotten over losing the house. It was the one that got away. Now, we were back, who knew for how long: displaced by a flooded bathroom in our rental in Mid-City, where we'd moved in the aftermath of all that loss.

Still, loss: isn't that what we were again encountering? Isn't that what this was all about? We'd been hustled out of our duplex so fast we didn't have time to pack. I'd discovered the water on a Sunday morning; by that afternoon, our bathroom was stripped to the studs. Now the management company was insisting on testing for mold and lead before rebuilding. There was other work they wanted to do. *A month?* the landlord conjectured, even as he acknowledged that he really didn't know. We'd spent three nights in a hotel before moving over here. The place was adequate—four small rooms and an eat-in kitchen. What it wasn't was ours.

I knew the neighborhood best from having driven through it. I knew it best from taking the kids to camp. Pico west to Robertson, where I'd turn south, passing the Robertson Branch Library, with its wall of quotes from, among others, Jorge Luis Borges and Oscar Levant. I've given up reading, the latter postured. It takes my mind off myself. It seemed a strange sentiment for a library, although it also made me laugh. Our children had gone to camp in Culver City; we'd pass under the 10, where one summer we saw a pigeon nesting in the traffic light at National Boulevard, then follow Culver Boulevard to Overland. If traffic was uncooperative, we'd take the side streets, which is how I came to know this corner of the grid. Los Angeles is strange like that, small communities tucked within the larger sprawl. This one was bounded by Robertson, the freeway, and, to the north, Cadillac Avenue: a triangular pie slice ten blocks long. You wouldn't know it to look at it. I only discovered it by consulting a map. This was part of the problem, or the challenge—that Robertson, a north-south street, angled slightly here, conforming to the 10 and Venice Boulevard, both of which bisected the neighborhood along a southwest tilt.

Our first full day on Olin, I woke early. I set out for a walk. This is what I do most mornings—looping meanders on a series of predetermined arcs. I've been a walker in the city since my childhood in Manhattan, when walking was a source of freedom...or, at least, autonomy. I brought the habit when I came to Southern California, a vernacular of the streets. Los Angeles confounded me when I arrived here more than thirty years ago; a key aspect of my acclimatization was to walk. On the most basic level, it was a strategy to find myself, by making the city small.

It didn't occur to me that this was what I was doing that first morning on Olin. It didn't occur to me that I had been exiled. This would come later, during the four-and-a-half months we spent traversing the city, from this Airbnb to another in Pico-Robertson, and then a third in Hollywood. It wasn't like being lost, or not exactly; we always knew, in some sense, where we were. All the same, how else to describe it? The dislocation felt as if it would never end. Each neighborhood was one I thought I recognized, although, of course, the opposite also turned out to be the case.

From the Airbnb, I followed Olin east until I reached the park. In the distance, I could hear the hiss of the 10. When we'd looked at the house on Hargis, the agent had tried to frame this as a selling point. It was like listening to waves break along the shoreline, he'd suggested, before telling us to consider a variable rate mortgage; after we demurred, he said that maybe we weren't committed enough. I knew it then, that we wouldn't get the place. I knew it then, that we would lose. Sixteen years later, I noted just how small it was. Unlike my wife, I did not regret being outbid.

No, all I wanted was to keep on walking. South on Reynier to Cattaraugus, north on Shenandoah, past the elementary school. It was early in September, so the term was already in session, although the hour was too early for teachers and students yet to have arrived. I continued to Cadillac, crossed Robertson at the light, and entered Beverlywood, where the street names changed, and the macadam looped or cul-de-sac-ed or had no outlet, as if this were a gated community without the gates. It was strange: for all the luxury on these blocks, the large houses with their sweeping vistas, the abutting stretch of Robertson was a desert—or the pandemic had turned it into one. The sidewalks were pocked with pitted storefronts. There was a Domino's and a Taco Bell, a coffee place or two, and a bakery. It didn't make sense, or maybe it was another contradiction. Southern California is full of them. All those years driving through this part of town and I had never really seen it. This was the Los Angeles conundrum writ small. A city experienced at thirty-five miles an hour will never reveal its nuances, no matter how much we imagine we might get to know them. In that sense, we are always lost when driving, always at a distance, always disconnected, disassociated: displaced in every application of the word.

This was why I walked, or one reason, to place myself within the landscape, to feel my presence in the street. I noticed details: the pet groomer on the corner, radio news murmuring in a low susurration from the back door; the way that, north of the park, Shenandoah narrowed until it became more of an alley, narrow and with no sidewalk. I didn't see a lot of pedestrians, and when I did, I kept my distance. The pandemic had left me wary of coming close. But this was part of walking also, that it allowed me to be

8:20
Your loc
Hamilton
ool
A
B
C
DONE

alone even as I moved through the city, that even as I navigated traffic and the occasional presence of other people, I could get lost inside my head. I wanted to immerse in my thinking. I craved the space of it, the detachment it required. I remembered the first moment I understood that no one knew what I was thinking, that my mind belonged to me alone. I was in first grade and the realization struck me like a bullet, or a method of release. This was what I did when I walked—to wonder furiously, to scheme and plan and settle. It had become a meditative practice in its way. In the world but not of it, as the Christians (or some of them) profess. Although I am not a Christian, I will admit to taking some comfort there.

The difference was that this was not my neighborhood. The difference was that this was not my home. In Mid-City, I would often proceed as if on auto-pilot, as if walking were a matter of muscle memory. An hour and a half would pass, and I would barely notice. I was just putting one foot in front of the other as I moved along accustomed streets. Here, I did not have that level of belonging. We had not been in the Airbnb for a day. As I crossed back out of Beverlywood, I was moving roughly east, or so I imagined. I was thinking about the work I had to do, and when we might go home. I was trying to catalog everything that seemed to be at stake. I wouldn't have said I was lost, although I wasn't paying attention...at least, not the right sort of attention, or to the necessary stuff. Then, I turned a corner and found myself on a small street that dead-ended against the freeway. I couldn't say exactly where I was.

I stood for a moment listening to the traffic. It did not sound at all like surf. After a moment, I crossed back (was it south or north?) to the lip of the street. I took a left on Garth and another one on Corning...and came face-to-face with the freeway again. This was not correct. But what to do about it? I was at a loss. I took out my phone, opened the maps app. It was there I found myself. I watched as I turned in what I imagined must be the right direction, but the blue dot that was me kept slipping away. I doubled back once more, to where Garth bled into Beverlywood. I knew where I was now but had no idea of how I'd come around. Passing Holt and Halm and Bedford, I could see parents and children walking in small clusters toward the elementary school. I had not expected they would lead me back the way I'd come.

When I first moved to Los Angeles, I used to get lost all the time. I would forget to turn while driving, and end up miles off my route. I would see a cluster of tall buildings and ask—the answer was almost never yes—if that was downtown. This, too, is part of why I walk here; let's call it a gesture of constraint. It's a matter of intimacy, in other words, of living out my private life in the city's public space.

And yet, cities do not belong to us; they have a life, a logic, of their own. If they are places where we may find ourselves, they are also landscapes in which we can get lost. All it takes is one wrong turn, one moment of inattention, especially on streets that are not unfamiliar, although not familiar enough. I was embarrassed, I'll admit, that this should happen in a city where I had lived for more than thirty years.

But this is how it always is, anytime we step outside the door.

ROAD SIGNS TAKEN FOR WONDERS

DANIEL LANZA RIVERS

It has taken me most of my life to learn to see the I-5. Despite being the portal to the family vacations of my youth, this lunar stretch of freeway has always struck me as a kind of absence made manifest. It's not what you think of when California's tourism website invites you to "find yourself here." Instead, this inland corridor of gas stations and khaki dirt is more like a messy staging area for the California Dream: a place where its fantasies of excess have let their wrappers fall to gravel shoulders and dusty patches of scrub.

I hated driving "the 5" when I started grad school. The six-hour trip from LA to the Bay Area stole a precious day of productivity, and it was usually bookended by commuter traffic of the most grinding kind. It would take me a few years for this resentment to soften, caving into resignation and acceptance after so many weddings and holidays and hospital visits up north. It's possible that I learned to expect less from the 5 during this time, but it's just as likely that the perpetual anxiety of graduate school forced me to revise my original assessment. To think of the road as a rare constant: an oasis of understimulation, which, if approached correctly, could offer me the kind of stillness I was trying to live without.

Sometime during the third year of my degree program, the 5 began to change. A drought had come on, and the road's tedium was sullied by a slow procession of signs. The driver heading north from LA encounters the first of these signs in "the Grapevine," a high-incline pass that climbs between two mountain ranges: the Tehachapis and the San Emigdios. Known to most Californians for its tendency to overheat engines, this leg of the drive edges along one of the largest consolidations of Mexican land grants in California's history. The parcel, now called Tejon Ranch, was amalgamated in 1864 after a particularly brutal drought punctured California's ranching bubble and made vast stretches of defaulted land available to settlers. The Tejon Company describes the product of this merger as "a California landmark, a land of legacy ... rich in history, blessed by nature," and boasts a suite of outdoor programs for wealthy vacationers. The company's promotional materials speak lovingly of Tejon's ties to regional history, all but erasing the land's connections to empire. Along with sidestepping the erosion of Mexican landholdings in the mid-1800s, the ranch's story ignores Fort Tejon's history as a site of bonded labor, illness, and starvation for Native people who were captured under

California's racialized vagrancy statutes. Tejon's mythmaking similarly erases the fort's role in surveilling hundreds of imprisoned Paiute and Concow people in the 1860s. As William Bauer Jr. notes in *California Through Native Eyes*, those Paiute and Concow people who rose up against settler encroachment in the Owens Valley in 1863 were forcibly marched from their homelands in the Sierra across 245 miles of dirt and scrub—with many dying and escaping along the way.

During my years driving the 5, I watched Tejon double down on its attempts to parlay historical fantasy into roadside revenue. First with dapper signage, then with the opening of a stucco-and-bell tower outlet mall situated on the Bakersfield side of the grade. This development hardly seemed noteworthy at first—after all, California is rife with mission-style homages to discount commerce—but it was soon joined by another parallel construction about forty minutes north on the 5, just off the exit for Kettleman City: Bravo Farms.

Where Tejon Ranch brings an austere approach to its historical fantasy, Bravo Farms mimes the Western stylings of old Hollywood. The southbound driver is apprised of its existence by a wooden cutout of a cowboy whose horse rears up as he aims his six-shooter at the sky. Those traveling north, by comparison, are greeted by a scarlet caricature of an Indian brave whose outstretched thumb is one-part hitchhiker and one-part soda jerk as he enjoins, "COOL PLACE CHECK IT OUT!"

Beneath Bravo's wooden exterior, you'll find a predictable mash-up of eateries, nonperishable fare, and wood shingles printed with aphorisms about laughter and the good life. There's a dog park, a wine bar, and a play area that reads like a schoolyard reboot of HBO's *Deadwood*. The exit to the parking lot abuts a giant slice of an old-growth Sequoia tree, whose somber magnitude offers an odd touch of natural history, while the copper buttons pressed into its rings testify to its ability to outlive Julius Caesar, Jesus Christ, and the Founding Fathers before being repurposed into commercial décor. Like so many of Bravo's offerings, this too strikes me as a fantastic anachronism: a locus of sensation and distraction that leaves a muted if bitter residue once I'm back in my car, packed up and pointed north for the many hours ahead.

Leaving Kettleman City starts the longest stretch of the drive. The novelty and fantasy that dominate the southern portion give way to a series of landmarks and tracts of emptiness so absolute you can drown in them. It's not uncommon for me to rehearse conversations during these middle hours, and fret over unfinished errands and bygone conflicts. Like many drivers, I mark my progress by the windmill outside Pea Soup Andersen's, the familiar rest stops, and the miasma of the Harris Ranch feedlot flooding in through closed air vents.

George Monbiot uses the term "ecological boredom" to describe a longing for biodiversity and complexity that can arise in a landscape that has been altered and simplified for extractive industry. This seems an apt description for the way this leg of the trip can shave away my patience, turning me numb and apathetic as I cruise alongside the aqueduct, passing so many signs for Fresno and Modesto, Los Banos and Mercy

Springs. "For Sale" signs and yellow placards decrying "CONGRESS CREATED DUST BOWL." Signs demanding that we get the delta pumps working, and signs that appeal to you with children's faces and logical fallacies about jobs going where water is flowing.

Despite my training in California's environmental history, it took me a year or so to look beyond the signs and see this stretch of the 5 as a landscape—with all the richness that term implies. I noticed the trash first: coolers and bumpers, constellations of broken glass and tendrils of shredded plastic waving in the wind. The orchards and pillows of tumbleweed came next, followed by the snaking aqueduct, the fog nets, and the hills that curve like the lines of a body. I noticed the fallow fields and upturned root systems of drought season, followed by the crayon sketches of yellows and blues when the rains returned.

The discourse surrounding California's water and agricultural woes may seem shrill and familiar to those of us who followed the news during this last drought cycle. Perennial as drought is, it sometimes feels more appropriate to think of California's water problems as a kind of haunting. The haunting both of the drought-adapted worlds that have been plowed under by empire, and of the fantasies of lushness and agricultural wealth that have directed two centuries of industry investment, technological manipulation, and labor exploitation on a grand, intergenerational scale. Like many Californians, I'm deeply implicated in these histories of water and agribusiness, both as a consumer and as someone whose genealogy is threaded with Central Valley settlers.

Agriculture is what brought my mother's Scandinavian and Danish forebears to the state, and it ran through all of my grandmother Marie's stories about growing up in Sanger, a small farming town east of Fresno. Born in 1936 to a father who did construction for the county and a mother who worked as a nurse, Marie remembers being put to work each canning season, as her family prepared the preserves they would eat through the winter. Like so many of her generation, her coming of age was crossed by World War II and the proliferation of chemical fertilizers, GMOs, and pesticides that followed the war's end and amplified the Valley's economies of scale. Throughout my grandmother's life, Central Valley communities were marked by economic disparity and social conflict, from the dispossessions of Japanese American internment, to the rise of labor movements led by Filipino and Mexican American workers, and the iterative attempts by grower's associations to demonize and disenfranchise California farmworkers—those most intimate partners of the land.

Driving this northern stretch of the 5 as an adult, my mind wanders toward that first spectral Valley, and the former lushness ensconced in the archives of settlement. Recalling his first descent from the Sierra into the Central Valley with a troop of surveyors, John C. Frémont writes, "It required all of our philosophy and forbearance to prevent plenty from becoming as hurtful to us now, as scarcity had been before." Writing in the "Bee-Pastures of California," John Muir calls the Valley a "smooth, continuous bed of honey-bloom, so marvelously rich that...your foot would press about a hundred flowers at every step."

And, looking back from a contemporary vantage point, historical geographer Gray Brechin offers an affecting portrait of the bygone landscape in *Farewell, Promised Land*, calling it "a vortex of life" and a crucial stop along the Pacific flyway where "two thousand antelopes came to drink at a water hole, and millions of birds congregated … to raise their young."

Driving the 5's khaki emptiness with these visions in mind, I can't help longing for that pre-industrial valley, with its deep water table, millions of migrating birds, and networks of drought-resistant fauna. The freshwater otters and seasonal lakes were so expansive that Spanish cartographers once mistook the state for an island. Of course, these visions are my own romantic approximations, another suite of settler fantasies that dramatize the 5 landscapes rather than facing them on their own terms.

Whatever has occupied me to this point, my thoughts always tend to drift forward during my final hour in the car, settling on emails and errands to manage when I arrive. I rarely notice the point where the 5 leaves me, splitting off to crawl toward Stockton and Modesto while I angle west toward the Bay. And the trip begins to blur behind me as I climb through the wind turbines and rolling hills of Altamont Pass, taking on the watery abstraction of a dream or a restless afternoon.

A CHUMASH LINE: HOW AN OLD EMAIL AND FIVE PDFS REVEALED MY NATIVE CALIFORNIAN ROOTS

MELISSA MORA HIDALGO

I.

The woman at the reception desk gave us a map and told us exactly where to go.

"Park by the utility shed near the Whittier Boulevard entrance here, in front of 579," she said, drawing our route with a highlighter. "Go four rows up and over to the right. You should find her here," circling the spot on the map, way in the corner.

We knew Calvary Cemetery well. We had visited the graves of other long gone Calzadas, relatives in my mother's maternal line. But today, we were nervous newbies. We were looking for a special Calzada, the one from the old newspaper clippings my auntie sent us in an email over ten years ago.

My mom, sister, and I dutifully followed the receptionist's directions. We found the shed, parked, and walked over gingerly, not just because of my mom's bum knee. I think we all had butterflies, anticipating something profound after years of talking with our mom's extended family and grandmother's relatives about our newfound Chumash roots. We stepped lightly, with quiet reverence, reading names out loud until we found hers.

CALZADA
Querida Madre y Abuela
Maria Antonia G.
Jun 13 1863 – Nov 11 1952

The three of us looked down at our ancestor's grave for the first time. Tears, smiles, laughs, hugs. My mom, sister, and I took turns saying hello, saying how happy we were that we found her. Our voices overlapped as we wondered things out loud, like who was Cipriano, the "Querido Hermano y Tio" she was buried with, and would Maria Antonia even know who we are?

"I'm sure she does, *m'ija*," my mom assured. But I felt the need to clarify, more for myself than for our ancestor. I needed to connect the dots, draw the Chumash family line that began in San Luis Obispo and ended right here in East LA.

"*Hola*, Maria Antonia," I said in a voice like I was in church. "We are your granddaughter Petra's family," I said. I shivered with goosebumps. "We are your descendants."

II.

Back in March 2010, I received an email from Auntie, who also sent it to my mom and their seven other siblings. The subject heading announced, "We are Chumash!!" Five mysterious PDF attachments accompanied her brief message. They were all labeled "Maria Antonia Calzada" and numbered one through five.

I had first heard of these "Chumash papers" two years before, when Auntie and Mom told me about their cousin in Ventura who used some of these documents to get her kids some kind of Chumash Indian scholarship. At that point, I emailed my mom's cousin to ask for more information, and she wrote back. She answered my questions but did not immediately send the documents. It would take almost two years for those "papers" to reach my auntie in 2010, when she passed them on, and my mom, her other siblings, and I would see them for the first time.

Auntie sent them to me thinking that I, too, could use them to get money for school. I was deep into dissertation mode by that time, one year from becoming the first PhD on either side of my big Mexican American family. I was also deep in grad school debt and always in need of financial aid or just plain cash. I could almost hear Auntie telling me, "Hey *m'ija*, check it out, you never know, our cousin did it. See if you can get a scholarship or something to help you out, *doctora*-to-be." Chicana Chumash power, *que no*?

Cashing in on a tenuous Chumash bloodline so I can finish my dissertation was one thing, and I felt a little guilty even entertaining the idea. Plus, as a Chicana, by definition I knew I already had "Native blood" of the Indigenous peoples throughout the land we know today as California, Arizona, Texas, Chihuahua, and Michoacán. My one direct ancestor, who by now probably had double the 268 descendants she left in 1952, I felt, was not necessarily going to qualify me for Chumash scholarships or anything of monetary value. That was fine.

But I did recognize these documents' historical value, and not just for my mother's large extended Calzada family. I knew what these five files meant to me as a California-born scholar of Chicana/o/x cultural histories and cultures, as a writer, and as a teacher in our public universities. One by one, I opened the "Maria Antonia" PDFs numbered one through five. Up popped news clippings about our ancestor, maps, photocopied pages from a library book, and a family crest. It was like a DIY version of *Finding Your Roots* with Henry Louis Gates, Jr.

Together, these five scanned pages represented a small but mighty archival batch of Calzada family stories and histories that place my mother's maternal line in California before the Spaniards invaded this land to build their missions, before Mexico "won" this territory post-independence, and before any Anglo-Americans showed up to dig gold from land that was not theirs. For us colonized Mexican Americans in the 2010s, these papers also raised a lot of other questions about ancestral indigeneity, land, borders, and the meaning of claiming "Native Californian Chumash blood" via our ancestor born in 1863.

III.

Of the five attachments my auntie emailed to us years ago, one page stands out. "Maria Antonia Calzada" PDF-One shows three documents photocopied together, arranged for context and chronology. At the top, a Spanish-language church bulletin from Nuestra Señora de La Soledad announces the funeral mass for "Sra. Maria Antonia Calzada, *a la edad de 89 años*," who passed away in Los Angeles, California on "Noviembre 11 de 1952." Under the funeral notice, two old newspaper clippings from undated and unidentified Los Angeles area newspapers, placed side by side, report the death of one "Maria Antonia Calcada." They couldn't even get her name right.

One headline shouts, NATIVE CALIFORNIAN, 96, DIES IN EAST LA HOME.

Another one simply says, BELVEDERE WOMAN DIES AT 96; LEAVES 268 LIVING DESCENDANTS.

The articles contradicted the church bulletin. Was she ninety-six or eighty-nine? Which dates were correct? Which newspapers are these articles from? And why was the death of Maria Antonia Calzada, my mother's great-grandmother, newsworthy in 1952 Los Angeles?

My mom, Auntie, and their cousins and aunts confirm that "the Church is right," that our ancestor, the "Native Californian" Maria Antonia Calzada (not Calcada), was eighty-nine (not ninety-six) when she died at the house on Zaring Street in East LA. She was born in San Luis Obispo, California in 1863, not in 1856 as the newspapers claimed.

The papers did get other things right about Maria Antonia. She married Pedro (my grandmother's grandfather, and her namesake) in 1880 at the Old Plaza (La Placita) Catholic Church, across from today's Olvera Street, although it was not clear when and why they left San Luis Obispo for Los Angeles. She had thirteen children; twelve survived. Her husband died in 1935 during one of their frequent trips "below the border" to Altar, Sonora, Mexico, where the couple owned a small plot of land. Maria Antonia's parents, Francisco and Maria Guerrero, were also born in San Luis Obispo, most likely what archaeologist and historian Rubén G. Mendoza calls "Mexicanized Indians, a "wholly new hybrid" as a result of acculturation under Mexican rule. Francisco and Maria became US citizens under the Treaty of Guadalupe Hidalgo in 1848, twenty-five years after the end of the Spanish mission period.

I never saw the word "Chumash" in either of the news articles, nor do they identify the name of Maria Antonia's "Native California" tribe or membership. PDFs -Three, -Four, and -Five included a few pages of Kroeber's 1925 *Map of Native Tribes, Groups, Dialects, and Families in California in 1770*, photocopied by our cousin in Ventura. They showed maps with lists that enumerated eight bands of Chumash tribes whose villages stretched from San Luis Obispo to Malibu. One map showed numbered parceled plots in and around San Luis Obispo. PDF-Two, which was a copy of the Calzada family name history and crest published by The Historical Research Center (1973–1980), explained the following: "The Spanish surname Calzada is of

local or locative origin, derived from the place where a man once lived or where he once owned land."

Where he (or she?) once owned land. Were we always Calzadas?

I went back to the email I kept from the cousin who did the research at Ventura College Library and the Mormon Church archives ("they keep really good records") to verify our ancestral line. And now I had the maps she previously described. According to records, at least three generations of Calzadas were born in San Luis Obispo between the 1820s and 1890s before they migrated south to East Los Angeles. According to our cousin, the land Maria Antonia, her parents, and later, her children (including Juan, my grandmother's father) were born on corresponds to area "14a" on the Kroeber map. "We located the parcel that we were pushed off of during the treaty [1848]," our cousin wrote via email on September 23, 2008. "It turns out that our land was what has now become known as Pismo Beach...and yes, we are CHUMASH.

Where we once owned land. Where we once lived. The border did more than cross us, I thought.

IV.

July 2019. My mom, sister, and I kneel at our ancestor's grave, just a few steps away from Whittier Boulevard and a mile from where she died on Zaring Street, in a house that no longer exists because it was razed by Caltrans in the 1960s to build the 60 freeway. We pull weeds, dust off dirt, polish the marble with spit and shirt sleeves. We brush ants away, a futile effort. Let them crawl.

"Imagine if we still had our land in San Luis Obispo, in Pismo Beach. Or in Santa Ynez or Los Alamos," I say to my mom and sister. I hear their murmurs, their agreement. "Yes, imagine, *m'ija*," and I do. What if the Calzadas were not pushed off Pismo Beach in the 1840s? Then other colossal "what ifs" flood my head. What if the *pinche* Spaniards never came and built their damn churches? What if there was never any Mexico or United States of America or militarized national borders or broken treaties, and Maria Antonia Guerrero and her parents, husband, children, and their children got to keep their land, their homes, their lives, their birthright, in their native California?

Who would we be? Who were we, before we were "Mexican," "American"?

At the end of her memoir, *Native Country of the Heart* (2019), Chicana writer Cherríe Moraga reflects on her mother's lineage and ancestral ties to the land of the San Gabriel Valley. Moraga's research revealed that her mother's Moraga family could be traced back to the "first recorded baptism of *'un indio' en la Misión de San Gabriel*," and that the baptismal register was signed by none other than *Fray* Junipero Serra in "the nearby Tongva village of Juyuvit" in November 1778. As Moraga writes, "This matters to me somehow: the proximity of Serra's ethnocidal signature, my maternal family name, and the Indigenous words for places I once knew as home. It is my own personal record that testifies to a complex system of mixed-blood, misnomered historical erasure."

Like Moraga, I am drawn to my mother's side and the indelible paper trail of our Chumash line that cannot be erased. I seek proof of our existence before we were misnamed, reborn as Spanish, as Mexican, as American. It means something to be able to draw a bold Magic Marker line between me and the woman whose grave we finally found, to connect these particular dots. Who needs DNA tests when we've got PDFs?

The Chumash part of my maternal grandmother's side represents but one branch of my proverbial family tree. "Your Nana Cruz was Yaqui," Auntie reminds me. "And your grandfather was from Michoacán," evidence at least of some kind of "Mexican Indian" ancestry. There is the mythical Nana Josefa, who they say was Russian and the reason why my sister and some of the aunties have light eyes, hair, and skin. This is just my mother's side. My father's El Paso/Chihuahua side—his mother's Cepedas can be traced all the way to 1520s Spain, as one *tío* did in the 1980s and 1990s before the internet made it easy—is a whole other story.

In 2019, the *Los Angeles Times* reported that there isn't a single full-blooded Chumash person alive today.

My sisters, our partners, and I often visit Solvang, Los Olivos, Santa Ynez, Los Alamos—towns in Santa Barbara County not too far from the Chumash reservation and casino. We celebrate birthdays, enjoy long teachers' weekends off, and mark important life moments together in those parts. My youngest sister even got married in Los Alamos, a testament to the power of the land and the meaning of our own ancestral connection to it. We feel it.

Chumash land calls us twice, maybe three times or more a year. Even though we grew up in the concrete suburbs east of East LA, the rolling hills and valley oaks and wine country roads up there feel like home to us because maybe, as Chumash descendants, it was once. It still is. Our spirits know that is our land, even if it is not ours in the colonial-Western-moneyed-private-property-real-estate sense.

At the grave, my mind drifts back to Auntie's email and the "Native Californian" in the newspaper clippings. When Maria Antonia Guerrero Calzada died in my grandmother's *tía*'s house in East LA in 1952, so the family story goes, did the last "full-blooded" California Chumash Indian on record. That's why her death was newsworthy, said my aunties and their aunties before them. (What is blood quantum anyway but a metaphor, another colonizing tool?) Whether or not she was the last one, my great-great-grandmother Maria Antonia Calzada remains my ancestral connection to our Chumash line.

HERE—AND THERE—LIES HOME

SAMINA NAJMI

Once, as a young teen, I found a poster of a brown, Western-looking house, with slanted roof and abundant springtime flowers, canopied by a blue sky. It didn't matter that those orange-and-yellow springtime flowers—tulips and daffodils—didn't grow in my hometown in southern Pakistan, or that our homes were made of concrete rather than wood. Nor did it matter that slanted rooftops never appeared on our urban skyline; we had flat, balconied roofs we could stroll on because, excepting torrential downpours during the monsoon season when water stood a foot high in the streets, it hardly ever rained in Karachi. What mattered was the ideal that the image projected, however removed from reality.

But I loved, above all, the English words that accompanied the image in slanted white print, as if sprouting among the flowers: Home Is Where the Heart Lies. It was the first time I had come across that expression. I purchased the glossy poster with my pocket money and had it framed in nearby Kamran Market. I intended it for my mother, on her birthday perhaps. On the back, I wrote in my best cursive: "For Ammi, the heart of our home," and encased the words carefully in the curves of an oversized heart. The framed image hung in our living room for some time before it succumbed to gravity, fell to the floor, and smashed.

I was twenty-one and still living at home like most young women my age when my mother moved out. She didn't move far physically, but she had outpaced her marriage and followed her heart where it led her. It was a brave, even scandalous, move for 1980s Pakistan, and because Ammi didn't seem like "that sort" of woman, people didn't know how to account for her actions except to say she might have taken to drugs. After all, opium abounded since the influx of Afghan refugees fleeing the Soviet occupation of their homeland, they said.

My younger brother's departure had preceded Ammi's; at sixteen, Amir left home in pursuit of the outsized dream of Stanford and called California home thereafter. My father, Abbu, my younger sister, Sadia, and I continued to live under the same roof until we sisters, too, answered the seductive call of America, cast in the ideal of a Western education. Ten years later, Ammi and her husband rented the house across the street from Abbu, and all of them lived as amiable neighbors for eight years until Ammi moved across town, the ocean beckoning. Abbu remained in our Karachi home—his home—until he died. He never married again. When asked why not, he'd say he wanted us to always have a home to come back to. Eight months after his death in 2013, Amir, Sadia, and I returned to Karachi for a week and sold the house that he and Ammi had purchased together, as its first owners, forty-three years earlier.

I have spent most of my American life in Massachusetts. But in 2006, the promise of a tenure-track position at California State University, Fresno, lured me westward. I was married then, with two young children, including a four-year-old son who sorrowed over the loss of the only home he had known. There was no way to tell him then that his was but the latest of multigenerational migrations in our family: from his great-grandmother's yearnings for Patna, in her native India, after the British-authored partition of the subcontinent in 1947, to his grandparents' attempts to belong in the London suburb of Greenford in the 1960s and 1970s, to his grand-aunts' and uncles' years spent in Denmark, Malawi, and Nigeria. His own mother's youth in London and Karachi, like her adult years in Boston, were marked by that twoness of home—the twoness that is sometimes the expansive feeling of belonging equally on two different patches of the earth; more often, the feeling that wherever you are, you hold on to one half of a whole.

This past summer, I worried how my son, fourteen now, would react to losing the second home he had known, the beautiful one in Fresno, with the adobe walls and red tile roof, the tall cypresses in front, and a pool in the backyard, clementines and kumquats to the east of the house, and lemons, grapefruit, and—most exciting to my parents—figs to the west. It was a beauty we could no longer afford; never could, really, but now as a single woman, I could make the decision to give it up without having to accommodate anyone else's dreams or delusions. Still, it was a hard thing to let it go, knowing I was not likely to live in a space that beautiful ever again.

But every time you move, be it 1,100 miles between Patna and Karachi, four thousand miles between London and Karachi, seven thousand from Karachi to Boston, three thousand from Boston to Fresno, or 1.7 miles from one home to another within Fresno—every time you move, you let go of some beauty. You let go of some ugliness. You hope that, in the end, beauty carries you over the threshold without your casting too many glances backward.

Backward, forward. The weight we give to those words: "backward" implying a retreat, submission, failure; "forward" always somehow better because the future is home to possibility. My friend Lucilia, who was born and raised in the Azores, once said she thought no one should ever leave home because there is no going back, even if you go back, and there is no moving forward without the weight of memory impeding your progress. There is no leaving behind your home. Or homes.

Sometimes at Fresno State, I teach Sandra Cisneros's story "Eleven," in which the child narrator says that when you're eleven, you're also ten, nine, eight, seven, six, five, four, three, two, and one years old, like the layers of an onion or a doll inside a doll.

I think when we live inside one home, we are also living in all the other homes we have ever lived in. We live among those smells, those surfaces, those different dawns; we breathe the air of those homes populated by faces we will never see again.

When my brother drove down from San Francisco to visit our old home in Fresno for the last time, I streamed a song for him by the Bangladeshi singer Runa Laila. The song, "Dil Dharkay," had been a hit in the summer of 1970 when our parents had moved us back from London to Karachi, a move that proved temporary because we returned to London in 1972, after the war with India and Bangladesh's hard-earned independence from Pakistan. Amir was not quite five years old at the time, but that day, his face brightened at the sound of the lively tune. He named the singer immediately and commented that she was a favorite of Chotepapa's, our beloved uncle who had blazed the trail to England, and who died the year my son was born. And then Amir startled me with the observation that, quite literally, the face of the map had changed since we first sang that song because East Pakistan no longer existed on the globe. As East Pakistan, Bangladesh had been Ammi's home, the patch of newly created Pakistan (which was itself envisioned as a homeland for India's Muslims, though most stayed in India) to which her parents had migrated after Partition. It was the site of her growth into womanhood, she and her sister together, in Bengali and Urdu and a smattering of English. And it no longer exists. It was wiped out in blood. The memory of that home is, for these two sisters, enmeshed with a memory of collective trauma on both sides of the violence.

As I write, I'm looking forward to my brother's first visit to my new home in Fresno, where we have been living for almost a month. Two intersections west of Fig Garden Village, it's a pretty, spacious, and well-located condo on Calimyrna Avenue that I have been able to buy with his help. My teenagers still have a pool, but without the worry of upkeep, because it's communal, and a tennis court to boot. Most glamorous of all for them is the proximity of Dutch Bros. with their boutique drinks, which has made our home a popular congregating point for their friends.

I look up the meaning of "Calimyrna" and discover that the word refers to the Smyrna fig as it is cultivated in California, in Fresno and the San Joaquin Valley where we live, in fact. Trace the ancient history of the fig and you find that it, too, has come a long way, a native of west Asia. It figures among the first plants ever cultivated by human beings—by some accounts, it may be the first domesticated plant of the Neolithic Revolution, some twelve thousand years ago—and it thrives even in inhospitable environments. Which is to say: it transcends time and space.

In California, it was Junipero Serra and his fleet of Spanish missionaries who introduced figs—the dark, so-called Mission figs—in the eighteenth century. The Smyrna fig, however, didn't find its way to California until the late nineteenth century, and it took another generation to figure out how to get it to bear fruit. In fact, figs are not really a fruit but rather inverted flowers that store their pollen inside. It turned out

Home is where
the Heart lies

that the Smyrna fig has to be pollinated by a special fig wasp from west Asia that lives inside wild "caprifigs." The tiny, two-millimeter female wasp has a symbiotic relationship with the caprifig: it provides her a home while she provides the pollen for the fruit. By a fascinating process, she is driven to leave her caprifig home in order to lay her eggs elsewhere. When she comes to a Smyrna fig, however, she doesn't realize that she won't be able to lay her eggs there because Smyrna figs have only female flowers. Spurred by instinct, the fig wasp is lured by the false promise of a home for her eggs.

But here's the thing: in the process of making her way through the opening in the fruit's crown, crazed by some desperate dream, her wings are torn. Once inside the Smyrna fig, there is no going back. So the fig wasp tries to go forward, from flower to flower, in vain. But no, not entirely in vain. According to author and natural historian Wayne P. Armstrong, longtime professor at Palomar College: "In her desperate attempt to lay eggs, she inadvertently pollinates the flowers." Inadvertently. Seeking one outcome and failing to secure it, she creates another. But "eventually she dies from sheer exhaustion, or old age." She's swallowed up by a protein-digesting enzyme and serves to provide the nuttiness and crunch of the Smyrna fig. Acre upon acre of fig orchards on Highway 99, just north of Fresno, testify to her enormous contribution to California's economy, and to the economy of the San Joaquin Valley, in particular. That's her future. The fig wasp is programmed to self-destruct for the sake of future figs.

The Smyrna fig gets its name from its homeland in Smyrna, present-day Turkey, where it has been cultivated for centuries. And the fig cultivated at about the same latitude in California becomes the Calimyrna fig in celebration of its dual origins: its present home in California and its ancient roots in Turkey, a country that itself straddles two continents on which I once lived. And yet the species is not a hybrid; rather, the Calimyrna fig traces a direct line of descent from those original cuttings brought to California from Asia well over a hundred years ago.

My daughter loved the condo the instant we saw it and has loved it consistently since. My son was won over by the time we moved in. I like it well enough and love it in moments when I see it through their eyes. It's ours, a home for just the three of us. True, my daughter will leave for college in almost no time, my son in just a little more than no time. But for a space in time, we will be rooted here together, and this Calimyrna condo will be home.

EL CORRIDO DEL COPETE

MYRIAM GURBA

The only reason I was sitting at the bleachers was because I wanted to watch this bitch get her ass kicked. This bitch, Karen, happened to be my neighbor. She lived behind a wall of pines, in a two-story mansion you could kind of see from my parents' biggest bedroom window.

Karen's pro-life mom drove a talking sedan, and in a robot voice, the car would condescend to passengers, nagging "Put on your seatbelt," whining "Door ajar!" I secretly hoped the car would kill Karen and her mother, and I learned of its existence when a few of us missed the bus, and Karen's mom chauffeured us to the front steps of the shit show known as Orcutt Junior High.

Kids who went to Orcutt lied. Most of them claimed they went to school in Orcutt, but according to the school's zip code, these fools really went to school in Santa Maria. I knew why they said Orcutt. Claiming Orcutt was a way of claiming whiteness, a coded way of saying that you lived in the "unblemished" part of town. The assertion distanced you from Santa Maria. Santa Maria was "over there." It was practically Tijuana: it was where "the Mexicans" lived.

Itty bitty Orcutt prided itself on not being Brown, and it styled itself as a low-rent Mayberry, replete with old-timey storefronts that gave the place a settler vibe. When I ditched, I'd stroll Orcutt, noting its stock characters: the toothpick-sucking old white man shuffling about in dark denim overalls, the skinhead zooming downhill on his skateboard, the Christian youth group leader drooling over thirteen-year-olds eating fries in front of Charlie's Burgers. On clear days, you could see the ocean from Charlie's. On even clearer days, you could see Casmalia, the toxic waste dump.

Karen wore the trappings of an oppressor. A pastel sock cascade devoured her cankles. Her denim shorts matched her denim vests. A scrunchie choked her half-ponytail into place.

Scrunchie girls were the worst, scrunchies signaled a commitment to adolescent fascism, and Karen unleashed her KKKalifornia girl kuntiness on me the afternoon we first exchanged "pleasantries." We were walking home from the bus stop, eucalyptus trees mentholated the air, and Karen eyed me like I was less than sirloin. The look gave me goosebumps, the ominous kind.

"What are you?" she blurted.

Dad had taught me to answer this question by declaring, "Chicana!" My intuition told me to keep it simple for my interrogator.

"Mexican."

"Are you sure?"

Karen's doubt took me aback. "Yeah. Why?"

"You have green eyes. Plus, you look Filipina."

I remembered the Filipinos I'd played tag and kickball with up until last year, sixth grade. One playmate, Ted Aguinaldo, even told me that I was a very good kickball player—for a girl. Ted's family worshiped at the same church we did, Saint Mary's, and Filipinos worked side-by-side with Mexicans in many places, including the hospital, the schools, and the strawberry and broccoli fields surrounding town. Santa Maria was serious about strawberries, so much so that we had an annual festival where we crowned a Strawberry Queen. Such was our aristocracy.

I wondered how the fuck Karen was such an expert on Filipinos given that she lived in Orcutt's whitest barrio: Lake Marie Estates. Yeah, I lived there, too, but I was, demographically speaking, the new non-white kid on the block.

"We had a housekeeper who was Filipina," Karen continued. "You look like her."

"Your housekeeper isn't my mom."

Karen kept staring at me, eyeballing my mustache, and I was on the verge of snapping, WHY DON'T YOU TAKE A FUCKING PICTURE?! when Karen's attitude changed. In a fake friendly tone, she asked, "Have you seen *Dirty Dancing*?"

I shook my head.

"Don't!" Karen barked. "It's satanic!"

Karen was finally saying something interesting.

"Satanic!" I echoed. "Tell me more."

Karen explained that since its plot involved abortion, *Dirty Dancing* was the Devil's film. Being twelve, I didn't know what abortion was. I did, however, know the word "abort," and I wanted to abort this interrogation, go to the movies, get refreshments, and sin.

Karen and the rest of Lake Marie's kids earned our distrust fast. Its preppy thugs welcomed us, the second Mexican American family to take up residence there, by annihilating our mailbox with a baseball bat, aiming what the sheriff determined was a pellet gun at our windows and blasting them full of holes. I'm almost positive it was Karen and her flat-assed friends who snuck onto our property the night of the pentacle.

"Myriam!" Dad hollered one morning. "Go get the paper!"

I hurried across our porch, past Mom's roses, and down our steep driveway. The paper had landed near a large agave. A mockingbird smiled at me from its perch, our new, still-intact mailbox. White caught my eye. I turned to see what it was and surveyed a dewy mess. Toilet paper mummified our oak trees and flannel bush. It draped the ceanothus Dad had planted along our hillside, and a wet glob of it crapped from a branch, splattering whiteness across the soil. I snatched the newspaper, looked up, and saw an epithet written across our driveway. Its letters were made of something white, maybe sugar.

Skirting the words, I sprinted to our front door, threw it open, and screamed, "Dad!"

Dad appeared in ladies' sweats. He preferred the variety of colors they came in. Wearing a worried look, he asked, "Is the mailbox still there?"

"Yeah but…just come look."

Dad followed me to the bottom of our hill. He surveyed our yard. "Shit," he said.

I pointed behind us, at the driveway. "Look."

Colorless letters spelled EVIL BITCH. Beneath the accusation was a sugary star held by a sugary circle.

Through his angry beard, Dad asked, "Who do you think did this?"

"The bitch with the talking car."

Ignoring my profanity, Dad said, "Go to the garage. Get the push broom and clean this stuff up. Also, please bring me my chainsaw."

I cleaned trees and shrubs and swept EVIL BITCH away while Dad found solace in cutting things up.

☀ ☀ ☀

I hated the gym, but I was in it anyway. The metal bleachers felt cold against my *pompis*. Down below, on the court, a boy dribbled a ball. Threw it.

He was not interesting.

Jenni was. I was focused on her.

Jenni was lighter-skinned than me but definitely not white. She was sitting in the bleachers facing ours, and she practically glowed.

All of the social rejects hanging out in the gym were there for her. We were TEAM JENNI.

Word on the street, and by "street" I mean our abusive-as-fuck campus, was that Jenni was going to discipline Karen. The bitch needed to be checked since she'd violated an important rule: Karen had shit-talked a *chola*. A Chicano, Freddy, had inspired the vendetta. Both Jenni and Karen had the hots for him, but Karen believed he belonged to her. She told everybody so. She also told everyone that Freddy deserved a classy girl, not a trashy whore like Jenni.

Now, because of her mouth, Karen might die.

I heard through the grapevine that to catch the violence, I should keep an eye on Jenni at lunchtime. After wolfing down tuna sandwiches, my friends and I spotted and tailed Jenni. She led us to the gym, and we played it cool. Nobody wanted to tip off to the administration that an act of guerilla barbering was about to take place. It excited me that the fight was going to involve hair and apparently, Jenni had told someone

who had told someone who had told a tall Mexican girl named Summer that Karen was going to get jumped. During the attack, Jenni would use scissors and abscond with Karen's dirty blonde *copete*.

I couldn't wait for the de-banging, the hacking of a nonconsensual mullet, and the promise of Karen's assault gave me hope: squadrons of Karens and Matts tormented so many of us at Orcutt Junior High and for once, the meek might inherit the campus.

Amidst a sea of white teachers, a solitary Chicano taught science. White girls gossiped that because of his Brownness, one should avoid being alone with him; he probably raped. And while shit-talking dark-skinned people was a popular campus pastime, woe unto those who talked shit in the righteous direction.

"Who do you think you are?" my white history teacher scrawled beside the F she wrote on an essay I'd done for homework. "How dare you write these things about Manifest Destiny?! Manifest Destiny is a sacred doctrine! It's why we're here. What do you suggest white people do? Move? There are too many of us! Your suggestions are very offensive and unrealistic!"

Our male faculty were worse. They watched and did nothing when white boys lunged, pointed, and hissed the n-word at my beautifully fat lips. Sneering at my mustache, boys groaned, "Ew. Yuck!" The worst of them jammed their hands between my legs, trying to rape me with fingers lubed by chip grease. They didn't hide their violence; it went down al fresco, and about once a week, marauders crept up behind me, grabbed my hem, and yanked my skirts up past my ribs.

One little gang turned my torture into a two-for-one. On their way toward me, they slammed a skinny Mexican boy against the wall, shoved their backpacks at him, and turned on me. Our audience froze. Once I was scrambling to cover my private parts, the predators sauntered back to the Mexican. After snatching back their stuff, the burliest one drawled, "Thanks, faggot."

My witness showed racial solidarity: he ratted my attackers out to our vice principal. Our vice principal told him nothing could be done about my constant degradation, but he was lying; something could be done. Lore I hadn't learned in school, lore I'd learned from books with bandits on the covers, pointed the way. These books belonged to Dad, they lived on our living room's bookshelf, and they clued me into stuff my white history teacher pretended hadn't happened. Gringos had been pushing Mexicans to the edge since they first trudged into California. Desperation turned us into desperados, and after they laid claim to our land, money, and bodies, they left us a single valuable to defend: our reputations.

From the moment I first saw her shuffle across our playground, I'd admired Jenni's walk. She moved pussy first, her clit was a bloodhound's nose, and Jenni dressed like my favorite gang-affiliated *prima*, la Green Eyes. Stretchy black jeans so tight her camel toe hung like lop rabbit ears. Nike Cortez. A black sweatshirt. *Si hacía frío*, a Raiders jacket cocooned her from neck to knees. La Jenni ratted and teased her locks identical to Green Eyes and her cynical baby face peered out through *un huipil grandote de tehuana*. Instead of lace and linen, the huipil's ingredients were Chicana hairs shellacked into place by Aqua Net.

(If you don't know what *un huipil grande de tehuana* is, picture a big-ass crunchy sunflower framing a *güerita*'s face. That was Jenni's hairstyle. I worshiped it. It is possible to worship hair, especially when it communicates aristocracy and reaches for the gods.)

Karen was watching Freddy play basketball. Jenni was watching Karen. She sat a few yards away from her, glaring at her hair. Karen felt Jenni's eyes and turned around. When she turned back, she was wearing a *fuchi* face. Once her eyes landed on Freddy, her *cara de fuchi* vanished. Adoration replaced it.

Jenni looked at her audience, at all of us gathered in the opposing bleachers. Slowly, she tugged her jacket's zipper down. By their handle, she pulled out a pair of large shears, displaying them so that they glinted. The spectacle stoked our bloodthirst. I trembled. I was on the verge of making *pipí* in my bicycle shorts. Anticipatory states often make me wet myself a touch.

Cluelessly, Karen stood. She smoothed her sweater. She adjusted her socks. She walked. Her best friend, Sarah, followed her. After they disappeared into the court-side restroom, Jenni smiled. She stood. An entourage of girls followed her. Tracing Karen's path, they entered the restroom. Those of us there for the reckoning held our breath. We feared tipping off grown-ups. This desire forced us to play it cool. My sense sharpened. *De repente*, a scream like a demon giving birth to a two-headed Medusa interrupted the basketball game.

Most of the boys playing froze. Freddy kept dribbling.

Jenni emerged. A worried crease lined her forehead. With her hands in her pockets, she scurried along the court's edge and flew out of the gym. Sarah tore through the restroom's doorway, flailing onto the court. She grabbed the teacher refereeing the game by his shirtsleeve and shouted into his ear. His eyes widened, and he shoved his whistle between his non-lips, blowing and blowing and blowing.

Euphoria filled me.

We had a hero.

* * *

During *mi niñez bilingüe*, two severed heads enthralled me. The first was female. I met it in Anaheim.

For vacation, Dad drove us to Disneyland and at the Haunted Mansion, we boarded Doom Buggies that spun us around a house filled with ghosts like in the novel *Pedro Páramo*. My favorite specter was nothing from the neck down. From the neck up, she was Madame Leota, a pretty dead clairvoyant. Her head floated in a crystal ball at the center of a round table, overseeing a séance, and Leota's makeup was spectacular. I wondered who did it. She had no hands.

The second head was actually several heads which had, and had not, belonged to Joaquín Murrieta. I'd learned about him, a Mexican bandit, from those books I mentioned earlier, and when I mentioned my admiration for Murrieta to Dad, he filled me in on a chunk of the desperado's tale that the books omitted: Murrieta's executioners had decapitated him so that they could collect the high bounty that the State of California offered for his capture. Afterwards, some enterprising *gabacho* tossed his head in a jar, pickled it, and charged people a buck to see it.

According to certain audience members, the head in the jar wasn't Murrieta's. Vigilantes decapitated the wrong Mexican, but really, aren't all Mexicans the same? Aren't we all bandits?

I'm a bandit.

The Mexican boy who watched my attack was a bandit.

Mom was a bandit.

Dad was a bandit.

My brother was a bandit.

My sister was a bandit.
Jenni was a bandit.
And because of that, the cops came and took her away. *La copetóna* never came back.
I would've paid at least a dollar to ogle her pickled piece of Karen.

* * *

The afternoon of the chopping, Karen didn't ride the bus home.
The talking car came and got her.
The bus felt different without her.
Lighter.
The kids who typically did the torturing, the white boys who spit on girls and called us hairy cunts, the white girls who sneered at those of us with "hard to pronounce names," acted a bit more reserved. Timidity had replaced viciousness.
I sat up straight in my seat, smiling, enjoying my ride home.
"This is how school should feel," I thought to myself.
The bus sped along Clark Avenue, across the 101 Freeway, and up a slight grade. I looked out the window, toward the Solomon Hills. Dad liked talking about them. In 1901, William Warren Orcutt had struck oil there, but that detail didn't excite Dad. What did was the legend of Salomón Pico, cousin of California's last Mexican governor, Pío Pico. Gringos killed Pico's wife, so to avenge her, Pico killed gringos. He ambushed travelers along the windy *camino real*, robbing them, dumping their corpses wherever he wanted to. Legend had it that he collected his victims' ears and my mind's eye conjured Pico resting in the shade of an erotic oak, humming to himself, petting his shriveled trophies, one or two still tufted with blood-matted blond hair.
The bus pulled up to my stop.
I disembarked Karenlessly.
I walked home Karen-free.

ADOLESCENT BLUES

RAMÓN GARCÍA

The girl interviewed on the local TV news was a student at Thomas Downey High School. It was the day after Mr. Hardwick, the eleventh grade English teacher, was gunned down on the front porch of his house. "It's hard to believe anybody would do such a thing. We're all in shock. He was such a part of our school. He was the nicest man, we'll miss him a lot..."

The girl recited the expected sentiments, the called-for clichés, as students seemed compelled to do, stepping into their roles of caring, shocked students. That's what high school life seemed to demand—assuming the roles that had been unquestionably determined, as if by fate. In this, high school operated like my Mexican family, in which each family member's behavior, strictly demarcated by age and gender, had long ago been decided.

The killers were shown on the local news channels being handcuffed by the Modesto police. Scrawny white boys with defiantly unfashionable hair that was too long for the early 1980s, they were hardly older than Mr. Hardwick's students, in worn Levis and T-shirts, their older brothers' hand-me-downs. They had barely distinguishable blank faces, inscrutably stoic—the kind of troubled poor white kids the Airport District abundantly spawned. They were set free after a short trial. I watched the reports on the TV news but never made out why they were not convicted.

The flag in the invariably green lawn of the school was set at half-mast, as it was every time a student committed suicide, died in a drunk driving car crash, or accidentally drove a truck into a canal and drowned. It was the official gesture of remorse, hence false, because no one mourned, no one actually felt sorrow; it was only the excitement of the sordid news, the lurid details of accidents or death, that were of any interest. Everyone knew the rumors: Mr. Hardwick was gay, rich, and attached to his mother.

I have not been able to come to terms with my memories of the murder, to understand the way the end of his life initiated the life that was before me. A lady TV newscaster with hair-sprayed, winged bangs recounted the details of the shooting as she reported from the suburban scene of the crime...Perhaps he lived with his mother... the mother is essential to who he was, the mark of his sexual identity. I was years away from reading Freud, but I had already picked up that male homosexuals were especially attached to their mothers; I was proof of that myself. But I knew I did not want to live with my mother for the rest of my life, which seemed to be the custom in Mexico.

At the time of the murder, I was in the eighth grade at La Loma Junior High School.

My older brother, Ismael, however, was a sophomore at Downey, and so I had already heard about him, the eleventh-grade English teacher, the gay teacher. Students at Downey passed down stories about Mr. Hardwick to their younger siblings at La Loma, so there were many kids still at La Loma who knew about him. We wondered what he was like with irrepressible fascination and requisite disgust. He inspired ambivalent interest because he couldn't or didn't care to hide the part of himself that made him… what? Dangerous? Vulnerable? A monster of rebellion? And so he had become a sort of legend, part of student lore.

The following year, when I was a freshman at Downey, Mr. Hardwick's murder was still talked about. The rumors refused to die, kept alive by the persistent interest in Mr. Hardwick's privileged, tragic life. Among the teachers at Downey, however, there was absolute silence about Mr. Hardwick, as if, for them, he had never existed. The only exception to the inexplicable silence was Mr. Mendoza, the ninth-grade English teacher. He alone partook of the mysteries born of Mr. Hardwick's gayness. Lecturing on Greek mythology, Mr. Mendoza, with a mischievous knowing grin on his face, his eyelashes fluttering, added, "Apollo was muscular and athletic, the Greek ideal, the kind that Mr. Hardwick would have been fond of." And the boys at their desks shot glances at each other, smirking, relishing Mr. Mendoza's indulgence in scandal.

In tight blue jeans and cowboy boots, Mr. Mendoza sashayed down Downey High's hallways with a questionable swaying of the hips. He spent weeks teaching us the myths of Ancient Greece—the deeds of the gods on Olympus, the fantastic legends of the Greeks—it was one aspect of his curriculum Ismael had liked. At home, eating tacos at the dinner table, he described the adventures of Odysseus, the hero's encounter with the sirens and the story of Medusa, the monstrous hag with snakes for hair. I couldn't wait to be Mr. Mendoza's student, to learn about the Greek gods from the book Ismael had passed down to me, Edith Hamilton's *Mythology*.

In his happy lecturing mode, puffing on a yellow #2 pencil, à la Bette Davis, Mr. Mendoza recounted the drama of the Trojan War and the violence and crimes of the house of Atreus. I loved his telling of the marvelous stories that lifted me out of my usual dejection. Eric, a friend in the class, who usually sat next to me, mockingly pointed out the obvious, "He's such a fag." And those within hearing chuckled. Eric had a talent for imitating the famous (Eddie Murphy, Johnny Carson, Jack Nicholson) and the not at all famous (people we knew), and he imitated Mr. Mendoza's faggy mannerisms when we loitered in the school's hallway in front of our lockers. Although we felt we could not admit it, we liked Mr. Mendoza; he at least didn't bore us. He amused himself as much as he amused us. He didn't censor himself as other teachers did, and that set us at ease; it opened us up to him. He allowed us to be cool, which is what we all wanted to be. We could ask him questions we would have been reluctant to ask any other teacher. "Do you smoke?" Eric wanted to know. "You act as if your pencil was a cigarette."

Mr. Mendoza smiled, confident in his comeback. "Well, it's healthier than smoking a cigarette. And it looks better." He was a regular Oscar Wilde at times. Mr. Mendoza took an interest in the arts, especially theater, and he was also a painter of sorts. Now and then, he was commissioned to paint murals and do set design for theatrical productions at the high schools in town. When he was entrusted to paint a "School Pride" mural in Thomas Downey High School's cafeteria, I was one of a handful of students he recruited to assist him. Every day, for more than a week, we stayed two hours after school to help Mr. Mendoza paint a mural that was to tower above the long tables where only the students who signed up for (or were assigned) government-paid school lunches ate—these were the newly arrived Mexican and Salvadoran kids who were still learning English, the few pale Russians who seemed to have landed in our midst from a distant planet, and the ambiguously foreign student, like the girl with hairy armpits who students said was Italian (she was "straight off the boat"). They didn't know any better; they weren't aware of the stigma attached to eating in the cafeteria. To eat cafeteria food on a tray at the cafeteria's long tables was to declare yourself a Downey High untouchable.

Our task as Mr. Mendoza's art assistants was to bring colorfully to life his mural-sized drawing, labeled according to the color it was to be painted, like a giant paint-by-numbers. Blue, in various shades, predominated, since it was the official school color and emblematic of school pride. The drawing, which would be a mural when we were through with it, depicted a glorious tableau of Downey High School Pride. In its center was a long-haired, buxom blonde maiden—a symbolic stand-in for the homecoming queen—riding atop a winged dragon. The Downey Duck (a humorous school mascot as opposed to the Downey Knight, the *serious* mascot) was drawn at her side, and below dragon and maiden, a burgeoning stew of puffy clouds contributed an Olympian touch. Pictured next to the dragon-riding maiden were a couple of knights in full knight regalia, representatives of the school's football team, the Downey Knights. We were kept busy painting the white of the clouds, the light blue dress of the Downey maiden, and the dark blue armor of the Downey Knights.

Rebel school groups like the Goths, the Heavymetalers, the *cholos* (not many, they went to schools on the west side), the Aggies (those who went in for farming and cowboy/cowgirl fashion), and the few Satanists (they wore black and hung upside-down crucifixes on their necks) didn't believe in school pride, and so were never seen during lunch hour pep rallies. Although cumulatively all the fringe groups added up to a majority, they were marginal in the school's cultural superstructure, and they felt it. Since I didn't fit in with any group, I felt it, too. My pubescent years were to be saturated in Downey High's various blues—the marine blue of football players' and cheerleaders' uniforms; the light baby blue of the school's hallways; the dark blue of hall lockers—a composite of blues that are the monochromatic palette of alienation.

As we painted away, Mr. Mendoza entertained us with Mr. Hardwick gossip. It was evident he savored talking about his dead colleague. "He got an autograph of Richard

Knight Scene
TDHS

Gere in Hollywood, at a movie premiere," he revealed. "I saw it. He showed it to me," he emphasized, as if to dispel any doubts we may have had. "It makes sense, of course, since Richard Gere is gay." Mr. Mendoza adored the movies and Hollywood history and was enthusiastic about gay Hollywood stars: Richard Gere, Marlon Brando, James Dean. He favored the stars of classic Hollywood—Bette Davis, Joan Crawford, Rita Hayworth, Cary Grant, Gary Cooper—they were just names to us, dead stars of a boring black-and-white AMC channel. All those big classic Hollywood stars had apparently been gay, too, like many of the Greek gods and heroes we were learning about in class.

It seemed to be true: Mr. Hardwick had favored football and basketball players whom he had showered with gifts, which implied there were illicit favors of a sexual nature in return. "Nothing in life is free, kids," Mr. Mendoza sophisticatedly underscored. He meant to shock us, but didn't. We were simply curious. I had the impression that he reserved the naughtier gossip for us, his art helpers, since he didn't touch such racy topics with equal openness in the classroom. One of these mythical athletes, for whom Mr. Hardwick had bought a Corvette after graduation, was playing football on a scholarship at USC, and his younger brother was following in his footsteps, playing on Downey's current winning football team, and no doubt heading straight to professional sports stardom. The school newspaper had done a huge spread on Stuart Mackey, this most consecrated of Downey Knights, who, like his brother before him, was being recruited by many college teams.

"They kept in touch after the Mackey boy graduated," Mr. Mendoza said. "He even went to see him play at USC, but I'm sure he got to play with him on his own." The younger Mackey, as athletically talented as his older brother, was equally popular. He was liked; he was handsome in a dirty blond, suburban way. A clean-cut preppy, in khakis and bright polo shirts, his tanned skin appeared incapable of sprouting a zit. Seemingly devoid of the unabashed smugness that was common to his kind, he was also supposed to be exceptionally brainy. He made the honor roll, was on the debate team, and God knows what else. He was so tall he made me feel short, yet he would smile at me in the hallways; he even winked once, which was shocking. No one winked. Winking was an absolutely unpracticed art at Downey and his little wink baffled me, left me reeling and puzzled. I knew I couldn't respond; I didn't have the confidence to even smile back, much less wink or say hello. He looked my way with tenderness and a telling, almost painful vulnerability in his eyes, hesitantly, but also flirtatiously. Stuart Mackey's warm smiles were inscrutable, since freshmen Mexican misfits and glorious junior WASPs did not normally acknowledge each other. He was evidently favored by the gods, a Greek hero reinvented for Downey High, and he had sent me a sign that came from another world. As Mr. Mendoza had explained to us in class, "the gods broke their own rules whenever they liked."

Atop tall ladders, as we painted the Downey Pride mural, Mr. Mendoza continued with what we already knew—that Mr. Hardwick was very close to his mother, a rich lady who spoiled him by giving him anything he wanted. "They went on trips to San Francisco together," he related. "They went to very expensive restaurants, to the opera, to the symphony. But I'm sure he went on his own merry little way when he put her to bed." His mother had so much money Mr. Hardwick didn't even have to work—but, Mr. Mendoza emphasized, he didn't exactly teach for the money.

Cheerful and odd, Mr. Mendoza had the dark skin and severely chiseled cheekbones of the Mexican Indian, but he was opposed to discussing his origins, or clarifying whether he was Mexican or not. Eddie, the only other Mexican in Mr. Mendoza's college prep English class, had asked him if he was Mexican. He defensively replied that it was nobody's business what he was, that it was "personal," meaning we didn't have a right to know. He claimed not to speak any Spanish.

In the evenings, I watched on the national TV news channels the unfolding story of a mysterious disease devastating gay men in San Francisco: sensationalist scenes of flamboyant gays cruising on Castro Street, quarantined hospital rooms, bathhouses forcibly shut down—the panic of a plague, broadcast in a righteous tone of fear and blame. In class, Mr. Mendoza touched on the scary new disease stewing in the evil gay lairs of San Francisco "You wonder if God is not trying to tell them something, warning them about what they are doing..." I didn't believe the retributional explanation for what would soon be defined as AIDS, but it still dug into my fears, into the consuming Mexican Catholic guilt I had been reared with. The guilt ate at my future with a vision of a sad homosexual life promising hell after death, and in between, if I was not careful, terror and disease.

It didn't help that in my efforts to get less biased, more educationally focused information about gay life, I came upon the Sisters of Perpetual Indulgence, the Radical Faeries, and the mustached S/M leather queens—an unholy trinity visited upon me late one night, when I stayed up to watch a late-night ("not recommended for younger viewers") PBS report on "Homosexuality in America." It was a sobering vision. The extravagant drag queens, the men dressed as nuns, the leather daddies wearing shorts tightened up the crack of their ass cheeks—they made me tremble with fear and sadness.

Did I belong to the same sexual species as the Sisters of Perpetual Indulgence and the men in San Francisco wearing leather chaps? I knew I could never be a "homosexual" like the homosexuals on TV. Or could I? Would I one day, inevitably and irremediably, turn into a freak? Was it my inescapable fate, the weirdness and horror broadcast from San Francisco? It was hard to imagine any of those outlandish, shameless San Francisco men on the TV screen had families that cared about them. I wondered if gay people existed who did not do strange, creepy things, like imitate Dolly Parton and dress up like nuns. But where were they? How did they live? And were they also dying? San Francisco, only ninety minutes away, seemed a God-forsaken place, a cursed Sodom and Gomorrah. And yet, I knew I could belong there, that I'd rather live there than in the suburban certainty of Modesto.

Mr. Mendoza, who in his person demonstrated a way out, so to speak, was not someone I could claim to imagine a future. By the time I was a senior, I would hear that he had gone heavily for the church. It was impossible to imagine him as a father and a husband, but that was indeed what he had become. On a visit home when I was in college, I saw him and his wife at the Vintage Faire Mall. He was carrying a baby in his arms, the first of many that were to follow.

The wife, in a dowdy, nondescript dress, plain flat shoes, and a white bonnet that held her hair in place, was an Old German Baptist Brethren Christian. I had grown up seeing, now and then, members of his wife's religion, the unassuming bland, passive-looking men and the mysterious children they were raising in their stern religion. They seemed a distant people, so austere and un-Mexican. And indeed, Mr. Mendoza's wife appeared colorless next to him. He seemed as content as ever, but his happiness was inscrutable.

During the blue years at Downey, I often thought about Mr. Hardwick. He was a Downey High ghost; he belonged to the past, yet he haunted my future. I had already decided I would search out the truth, accept who I was, since denial seemed even more empty and impossible. I figured my life was a unique purgatory no one else in the world had ever been placed in, and the best I could do was get good grades and search for an out—or I would simply not make it.

My real life was somewhere beyond the flat horizons of the San Joaquin Valley, to be realized in college, perhaps, in adulthood, in books and love and writing. Sex was a dark continent—dangerous, unfathomable territory, but I would have to go there, even if I stayed away from San Francisco. I would have to explore, among the land-mines of AIDS, because otherwise it was the equivalent of dying, of not having lived. I could be myself, I hoped, and not necessarily accept tragedy as my lot. At the very least, there was survival. If truth didn't triumph, which seemed very probable, then survival was certainly better than living a lie, or being a ghost.

SHOWCASE THEATRE, CORONA

CHRIS GREENSPON

March 12, 2006. My second big punk show. The Adicts at the Showcase Theatre in Corona, California. Way the fuck away from my home in La Puente.

I was supposed to see them a week prior, not too far away at the British Invasion 2k6 at the Orange Pavilion in San Bernardino. The show got shut down after I had been there for two or three bands. A skinhead demonstration had led to a stabbing, tear gas, looting, and riot police. I was fourteen.

My dad had been nearby listening to KFWB in his old Datsun, heard about what was going on, and came back and swooped me up. I was extremely disappointed to have missed The Adicts, essentially the only band I came to see, until it was announced that they were playing another show a week later, for half the price. I took a flyer with me to school. The older, hippie punks I knew, who had claimed to smash a cop's windshield that night, said, "Oh, it's at Showcase." They didn't seem too surprised and smiled slightly.

At what? At where? I had only heard of punk shows happening in backyards in the San Gabriel Valley, clubs in Hollywood, and this lame coffee shop in Azusa called Smart City Grinds where Cheap Sex played once. The bell rang and I headed to class while the hippie punks returned to their hacky sack game.

It seemed like all of a sudden, the Inland Empire was the place to be, before I even knew of its reputation. In my mind, that's where Mexican and white punks gathered in mass numbers, stood together against fascists, smashed fast food restaurants, and where The Adicts played whenever you wanted to see them.

I pleaded with my father to take me again. This time, he wasn't just dropping me off. Two tickets it was, and a ride down two freeways I'd never heard of.

We drove out from La Puente on the 91 and the 71 freeways on a school night. My dad excitedly reminisced about visiting his aunt in Corona in the early '60s, riding minibikes in empty fields, and eating hamburgers at Hi Spot. It sounded like some redneck shit to me.

We got off on Main Street and arrived to what seemed to me like flat-in-the-middle of fucking nowhere. A Del Taco to our left, a 76 gas station to the right. Despite some charming old buildings and a curving line of trees, the place felt somewhat sad. It was getting dark in downtown Corona.

We went another block or two, past the city library, and then I turned my head to see hundreds of kids surrounding a frumpy brick building next to the 99 Cents Store. It was like they had taken it over.

We parked beside some girls hanging out in a blanketed truck camper, slyly drinking forties. My old man seemed more accustomed to this kind of scene than I was (after all, he saw The Doors in the '70s). As we walked up to the building, he snapped a picture of the building's cheesy marquee: Showcase Theatre.

The parking lot was alive with girls and boys with blue and pink hair, spiderweb tattoos, painted leather, and cheetah-print everything. They screamed at each other and played grab-ass, while the older ones smoked cigarettes. There were a few middle-aged people there, too, just as punk as the rest.

This Corona was redneck shit indeed, and my sheltered Mexican mom-having adolescent self was about to get his first taste of it. I met a nineteen- or twenty-ish-year-old guy whose name I don't remember. He had the tallest spiked hair I'd ever seen and the most thrashed, moldy Cramps shirt. It gave those hippies at school a run for their money. He said he lived around the corner. I asked if he came to all the punk shows. I had just become aware of hardcore, metal, and "scene kid" music and eyed it with distrust. He said he came to Showcase Theatre every night, no matter who played, just to fuck around. He made eye contact with the tallest, scariest bouncer and called "Waddup, Big Ron?!" Big Ron's scowl turned into a huge grin.

At seven o'clock sharp, the bouncers snapped into authoritarian mode and shouted us into lines. Everyone mostly complied. When I got to the box office window, ringed with stickers and faded graffiti, a middle-aged blonde woman with Coke bottle glasses and a green cardigan asked me, "Tickets or will call?" Not understanding the question, I blinked at her. She sternly repeated herself and then gave a look to a Mexican goodfella in skate clothes standing by the door. He told me to empty my pockets, took my ticket, and sent me inside. He was the club's talent booker and stage hand, Joe Case.

I felt like Bilbo Baggins entering the back door of the Lonely Mountain under moonlight. There was a dark hallway covered in posters for upcoming shows: UK Subs, The Meteors, Avengers. It was probably only twelve- or fifteen-feet-long, but it's burned into my memory like the slow pan-up at the beginning of a movie that takes place in a Chuck E. Cheese for punks.

Traffic lights and an old bicycle hung from the ceiling. There was a small, round stage, no more than three-and-a-half feet high, flanked by huge speakers, and a little cage next to it for the sound guy. The wooden dance floor in front of it was soaked in years of sweat and framed by a squared, corral-like rail that separated the pit from the loading ramp, the entrance, and the snack bar with its Christmas lights. The old crust punk *tíos* and lifers leaned up on the rail with slushies and popcorn while their young ones ran up and down the staircase to check out T-shirts and CDs on the balcony. Underneath the balcony was the chill out—or make out—area. Behind the snack bar, past the world's loveliest bathroom, was a red Naugahyde couch, arcade machines, and a water fountain that never worked.

The show started quickly. My pop and I went up to the balcony to watch the opener, The Giggaloops. They were locals, mostly girls, four or five years older than me, and they were playing their last show ever. First song and the kids were already pitting and singing along. I couldn't believe a band this young had a following and could open for legends like The Adicts. I think one of their moms might have worked in the snack bar. I was enamored with their lead singer's pin-up style and cool vintage microphone. They thanked Showcase numerous times—that's what everyone called it, Showcase—and when I got their free CD later, it had live tracks recorded there that actually sounded better than their demo.

The Adicts, as I would find out, played the Showcase many times a year. It was where they had made their return from hiatus in 2002, before they moved to California. They'd released several records with a label cofounded by the venue's owner, Ezzat Soliman. These British legends made Corona their home base and were huge in SoCal. The tight confines of the club (capacity 450, I think) gave the perfect conditions for the band to explode confetti and throw out beach balls to a swaying crowd of teenage heathens.

After that first show, I kept making the trip out to Corona any chance I got over the next two years, meeting new friends, eating the pizza next door, and pissing off the 99 Cents store staff. I saw more and more that the Showcase had its own scene of artists who were making (or trying to make) their careers in music, largely off the opportunities that this little place and its community afforded. Not only was it the spot to see Vice Squad or TSOL, but there were hordes of young people honing their chops on locals-only bills that were generously provided by Joe Case and Ezzat Soliman.

The stereotypical skeezy Inland Empire element was there. I remember a middle-aged, leather-faced crew called the Runt Punx. They had names like Spit and Weasel and dressed sorta like GIs or Gestapo. One of them slapped my best friend Garrett in the titty as we crossed paths in the doorway. Boy, was he pissed. The Corona City Bootboys were a skinhead group that came out and busted up a D.I. show. I once saw a methed out guy who looked like Matthew Lillard push a revolver in a fresh-cut baby skin's face and ask him if he wanted to "play with bullets" while the kid pleaded, "I'm not a fuckin' Nazi, man. Please don't shoot me, I'm not a Nazi, man!" This happened about a block south of the club. My sister and I watched with bewilderment from the bushes.

But I met a lot of artists and intellectual types there, too: a family with a record label whose kids ran food drives and became train hoppers. A guy from Temecula who printed Patti Smith and other poets on his shirts. All the photographers. Of course, there were all the politically minded bands and fans spreading messages about police, war, and animal rights. And just a lot of friendly people who loved to dance and didn't mind getting crashed into.

I'm not totally sure where everyone came out from, and how many people were Corona locals. Many came from Riverside, where the Showcase's predecessor, Spanky's, resided in the late '80s. Garrett came out from Rancho Cucamonga. Recently I learned that my cousins, who had moved from Alhambra to Ontario to Mira Loma, had gone to Showcase with their aunt and gotten drunk for the first time in the parking lot. All the while, the IE felt like such a nebulous region to me.

In 2008, the Showcase shut down pretty quickly. I didn't know what exactly happened—a lot of pressure from the Corona City Council apparently—but I had gotten my taste of what punk rock was supposed to be, and spent many more nights in search of it in backyards in the SGV, galleries in Echo Park, and bars in Orange County.

As I ventured further into rock scenes enabled by the bull economy and gentrification of the Obama years, the happy times I spent in the circle pit at the Showcase didn't feel quite as hip. I drank in some of the highbrow, anti-hick, and apolitical sentiments that swirled around some of the more affluent garage rock and art punk shows. Showcase wasn't a place I brought up anymore, and I'm ashamed to say I even cringed a time or two when my father mentioned it years after.

More recently, I just about completely lost interest in the bulk of what goes on in the LA rock scene, as even the bands who are supposed to be super punk mostly just play in clubs with sideways fences that seem to have been built to serve as backdrops in commercials. Everyone's gotta make a buck. It's not to say something isn't happening somewhere that means something to someone though. In fact, geographically, I started to notice something funny.

Maybe it was just nostalgia that caught my peripheral vision, but I started noticing that old school punk, with all of its trappings, still exists in the boonies like Corona. Marla Ríos-Hernández's dissertation on punk made the papers. A gigantic fair for punk street vendors was happening yearly in Upland, until COVID. And Alta Loma's Dr. Strange Records is still going strong twenty-two years later. I hadn't seen an honest-to-god punk family walking the street in the SGV in ages, until I went to see Logan Colby's 2019 documentary *If These Walls Could Sing* at the Concert Lounge in Riverside. It was a rowdy and emotional evening. The audience cheered younger versions of themselves jumping off the stage, as the Soliman family sat tearing up in the back row.

Now, many years since the Showcase shut down, the Inland Empire has taken on a clearer identity in my head. It's a place without pretense, where people do what they have to to survive and thrive. The IE, and Corona, are punk.

OH, SALINAS!: SONG, STORY, AND PUNK ROCK BEHIND THE LETTUCE CURTAIN

GEORGE B. SÁNCHEZ-TELLO

The long white buses are unmarked. The paint job on the bus panels looks thin and cheap. If I stare long enough, I could probably make out the name of the school district or church or factory under that white layer of cover. The buses idle in an empty parking lot that is pockmarked with potholes partially filled with mud, water, and a slick oil sheen. The gravel is crumbling. In the distance, mist hovers over the fields.

The people boarding the buses stand in single file. Their informal uniform consists of jeans and sweatshirts, baseball caps, bandanas, and other shards of cloth fashioned into face masks. The buses will carry them to those fields. Soon the workers will be silhouettes in the distance, bent over and picking, working themselves up and down the rows of lettuce, strawberry, and spinach.

Every one of them has a name. A home they come from. A language they were born into and another adopted for work. Most of those people have children. I always wondered who they were and what their stories were. None of this is new. There was no "news peg to hang it on," as an editor would say. So I wrote a song.

> In the pre-dawn dust of the parking lot the workers form a line
> They board the long white transport bus and hope the kids are fine
> Left home alone with the little ones
> The cousins will take care
> Mom wraps a T-shirt around her face to filter out the filthy air
> No food to wake the little ones
> Pop-Tarts will do just fine
> Gonna make do with what we got
> Gotta stretch every single last dime
> Why?
> 'Cause that's where we're at

A few miles away, on a given Friday night, the children of those workers sing along. In a small café or the backroom of a Mexican restaurant, bodies pack together, in their own uniform of jeans, faded black T-shirts with band logos, jackets or vests quilted with small square patches. Everyone joins in to sing:

> Another song about the Salad Bowl
> About the place that we live
> This valley can be a prison
> Just ask the kids!

"Where We're At" is a song I wrote for Rum & Rebellion, a punk rock band from Salinas, a farm town in Monterey County on California's Central Coast. We were one of many: from Salas, Chole, Prunetucky, Watson, and King City. We played in cafes, backyards, apartments, community centers, storage sheds, bars, restaurants, parking lots, and clubs.

Rum & Rebellion songs were a refuge for stories. A place to safely express my voice—literal and literary. During the day, I worked as a newspaper reporter, first for the *Salinas Californian* and later the *Monterey County Herald*. I often wrote newspaper articles about crime, education, and local politics. I wrote songs about what I witnessed: the tired *paletero*. The teenager walking to school. The father of a lifer. The *campesino*. Portraits of the people, stories, and moments between me and the farm fields that surrounded a town known for labor, E. coli, and, of course, Mr. Steinbeck. What was otherwise the setting in an article became a story in a song.

For being a small farm town, Salinas has a population of about 150,000, making it the largest city in Monterey County. Someone once said the population doubled during the harvest season. Of course, it was exaggeration, but the harvest—or more like the people harvesting—was inherent in all aspects of life in Salas. Education officials coordinate with districts in Washington and Arizona as families migrate to work the harvest elsewhere. The school districts start later in the winter to account for families returning from Mexico. For many years, the town was segregated: whites to the west, Mexicans to the east, or the Alisal, as it was called. The annual Cesar Chavez march is not a relic from a Chicano Studies class, but a testament to community, organizing, and the continuing ability to mobilize in support of one another.

Not all Rum & Rebellion songs were high-minded: I wrote about crushes on an older woman and colleagues. And drinking.

I wrote angry responses, as in the song "No Charity":

> Don't need no charity
> Got my own pair of lungs
> There are no voiceless
> There's only repression

And songs—“Hey Armando!,” “No Folk Song (New DA Blues),” “Not Down”, “Four Years”—about prisoners. All of whom I’d met and spoken with.

If there was a news peg, I filed an article. But the daily, almost taken for granted, became song. I think one of my favorite compliments of Rum & Rebellion lyrics was the disappointment from one person after she learned I was from Los Angeles and not Salas.

Rum & Rebellion came together after a freelance assignment for *Punk Planet*, one of the national punk ’zines at the time. Scott MacDonald, a photographer for the *Salinas Californian*, and I spent a weekend with Against Me! and Lucero. Scott also played drums. I could play guitar. I could write. And yell.

As a reporter, there were stories I carried with me, stories I’d witnessed, that would never get past my editors. Like the quiet dignity of *campesinos* lining up for work in the early morning: a sight so familiar in East Salinas it had become a regular backdrop. Or the ritual of family members waiting in line outside county jail on visiting day. Stories that required more nuance than I could fit into a twelve-inch print article. Or stories that required a different worldview than most of the papers’ readers and editors had.

There were subtle reminders, like the “News From Home” section that carried articles from the Midwest. Maybe it was because I was from Los Angeles, and I had plenty of coworkers from other parts of California, or simply knowing home for many in Salinas was Mexico. Sometimes they were blatant: like a red-faced, irate white editor telling me “Everybody knows Latinos are the most macho people.”

I can’t pin it on a single editor, though there were certainly a few who reminded me. Because I learned lessons about what to share and what to withhold long before I became a writer. Lessons about the sense of security in silence. Lessons learned by parents who, in turn, transmitted them to me. Lessons of “Americanization” taught by the Sisters of Loretto across the Southwest two generations before my birth. Lessons of silence wrought by the onset of the Guatemalan Civil War. Lessons of hiding in plain sight after my family arrived in Los Angeles after the mass deportation of Mexican and Mexican Americans during the Great Depression. Lessons of obedience when my father began working for the Los Angeles Police Department. And the lesson that no matter how I spoke, what I wore, or where I lived, I’d never fit comfortably into an affluent white suburb.

When I wrote my entrance application essay for Saint Francis High School, I took seriously the invitation to write about someone I admired. I wrote about Steve Clark, Def Leppard’s founding guitarist. I still go back and forth about whether that was one time when I should have kept a story to myself. By the time I wrote my entrance essay for Loyola High, I had “learned” better.

As a reporter, I had my own uniform: I wore a collared shirt and necktie. With my black-and-white Doc Marten brogues, I had a distinct, pachuco-inspired style. But it was still a shirt and tie. A shirt and tie I wore purposefully to access what Nolan

Cabrera calls "white immunity," or the protection from disparate treatment. Day in and day out, sitting on the press bench in a courtroom, I couldn't help but notice that the people who looked like me also wore uniforms: either orange jumpsuits for inmates or the green and khaki of the sheriff's deputies. Those with ties were attorneys, the judge and, on the rare occasion, a defendant. And me.

I learned to wear a tie at Loyola, an all-boys high school. By that point, I had learned to be careful of what I said in front of whom. To be aware of authority. Eventually, writing became the place where I could express myself freely.

When my editor caught a Rum & Rebellion acoustic set at the Cherry Bean and he asked me to write more articles like my songs, I appreciated the compliment, but I couldn't simply shrug off the decades and generations of learned and practiced silence. Thankfully, there were those who wouldn't remain silent.

Touring punk bands typically bypass Salinas, heading north to Santa Cruz or San Jose. The exception were those that were connected through the Razacore network of punks who could put up bands and shows in farm towns outside the bigger cities. Thanks to Eduardo of the band Outraged in Watson, Limp Wrist came through. Argentina's Boom Boom Kid did a show in Salas. But there were two bands—La Plebe and Los Dryheavers—with roots in Salas who always returned from San Pancho and

San Jo to play periodically. Those shows were the best.

Salas punk shows meant fifty to a hundred young, sweaty bodies squeezed up against the walls, counters, and the band itself.

Shows with booze were at the Penny, an English pub, and all-ages shows were up the street at the Cherry Bean, a local café.

When the Dryheavers played, the guitarists, bassist, and singer encircled the drummer. They usually had to play with their backs to the crowd to ensure the space to strum and, in the singer's case, make sure the crush of the crowd didn't lead to teeth getting knocked out.

There is a story about Los Dryheavers. It is too good to ruin by finding out if it's true. Los Dryheavers "played" the Warped Tour. Except Warped's Kevin Lyman didn't invite Los Dryheavers. They simply packed up their van and drove along with the Warped caravan. At each stop, Los Dryheavers set up outside the festival and played. With the exception of Kory, all the Dryheavers were big, heavy Chicanos. Not even Warped security wanted to bother them, or so the story goes.

One Salas show, in between songs, Los Dryheavers's singer, Hector, took a moment to speak. First, he needed to catch his breath. Not uncommon.

"My family works hard. They work the fields, like your families," said Hector, slightly gasping from screaming and trying to breathe through the humid air thick with sweat and body odor. Hector turned to Felix, one of the Dryheavers's guitarists, and asked what his parents did.

"Big pimpin'," he responded.

The sudden pivot from vulnerable self-admission and statement of solidarity to crude humor: I laughed. That was Salas punk—irreverent, political by imposition, and impatient for the next song. It was Chicano Punk Rock. It was Immigrant Punk. It was Los Dryheavers, La Plebe, Outraged, Uzi Suicide, the Gunslinger, the Kings Kids, Dear Avarice, the Achievement, Cali Nation, Bound to Break, Madtown Mulligan, Darktown Rounders, Chainsaw Death Squad, Toxic U.S., and so many others.

ACTS OF GRACE: MEMORY JOURNEYS THROUGH THE SAN JOAQUIN VALLEY

BRYNN SAITO

Places are alive like ghosts are alive: subtle, unpredictable shape-shifters, infused with memory and emotion. The spirit of a place—the *genius loci*, as the ancients called it—rises from the land's stories, its unique matrix of weather, struggle, celebration, and blood. There are places we return to again and again to find our stories. We change; they change. The stories we tell take on lives of their own.

The story of my Korean American and Japanese American families begins in Dinuba and Reedley—two rural towns in the heart of California's agricultural basin, each about thirteen miles east of Highway 99, which runs midway between the Pacific and the Sierras. Sometimes, the tale begins in the aftermath of war and incarceration: my father's parents, Alma Teranishi and Mitsuo Saito, returned to California to resettle in Reedley after their release in 1945 from the Gila River concentration camp in southern Arizona—the place where they met, married, and gave birth to their first child. My mother's father, Samuel Oh, returned from the European frontlines to his hometown of Dinuba where a divorce awaited him—a separation that, ultimately, set the stage for his meeting and marrying my grandmother, Marilyn.

Sometimes, the story begins earlier than that: the first generation arriving on Angel Island, then laboring their way to the southern San Joaquin Valley—a place that would, over the course of the twentieth century, become the source of twenty-five percent of the nation's harvested food. Almonds, olives, stone fruit, citrus, vegetables, berries, alfalfa, winter wheat: crops planted and picked by migrant and immigrant workers, generations of laborers making their lives in the shadow of the distant Sierras.

On a gray, post-rain November morning, I travel with my folks from our home in Fresno back to Reedley and Dinuba. Rows of vine fruit wind along a diverted Kings River and mountain slopes sport majestic, white-painted letters signifying small farming towns: the "R," the "S," the "D." We visit the church where my mother grew her faith; the stadium where my father captained his high school football team; the side lot location of the tree my father and his older brother set fire to—with a boy still in the branches (who, luckily, survived the prank); the old home, where Dad's dad carved, in their front yard, a stone pond for koi.

What follows is a reflection tracing the morning's journey.

"In the summers, your dad used to run barefoot through the streets to get to the town pool," says my mother as we drive the streets of Reedley, my father's hometown. I imagine Dad young and running, his little-brother spirit, his charming, mischievous smile—all of the energy of someone totally beloved by his mother, occasionally scolded by his volatile father, teased by his older brother. High school football captain, eventual PE teacher, basketball ref, football, basketball, track, and golf coach—and trainer of two, lazy teenaged daughters: I remember my dad up at dawn, cheering us into shape. At seventy-two years old, my father still runs—many miles each week in the morning's winter cold. My father has been running his entire life.

There are close to twenty churches in less than two square miles in Dinuba. My mother came of age in the Dinuba Presbyterian Church, now the Iglesia Nueva Esperanza. Graced by palms and *Pistache* trees, the formidable building towers above us, as we wander along K and Merced Streets. My mother's grandfather, Tai Eun, fled Korea for America at the height of the brutal Japanese occupation, eventually establishing himself as a lay leader in Dinuba's tight-knit Korean Christian community. After it disbanded, my mom and her two brothers started their Sundays at Dinuba Presbyterian, a mostly white congregation. In her day, the Korean American population in Dinuba was larger than in nearby towns, though much smaller than in urban centers like LA or San Francisco. As the decades passed, my mother's faith continued to anchor her—eventually, she became a lay leader in the Japanese American Christian church (a story for another essay). "Mother, I watch," begins a poem I wrote for her. "Strong, you walk tall reflecting mountains. / Water grows more sure of its strength as rain rushes beneath / cool elm winds. / You are not / anymore a shard; history's strong song makes us whole."

Dad, storytalking in front of the Reedley Buddhist Church on 15th Street, the church where he was raised. The story of Buddhism in North America reaches further back than the zen and meditation movements of the 1970s. First-wave Asian immigrants in the early twentieth century brought with them Buddhist belief systems rooted in the Jōdo Shinshū, or "Shin" (True Pure Land) tradition—the tradition of my father's family. The Reedley Buddhist Church was built in 1936, then rebuilt in 1952, after the wartime incarceration of the West Coast Japanese American community. Neither my father nor I remember what exactly he was pointing to beyond the church gates—most likely, a story of some prank or mischievous behavior—though I do learn that, as a young person, my father was the president of the Young Buddhist's Association (YBA), the youth group of the Buddhist Churches of America. Both of my parents were shaped early on by spiritual traditions anchoring the lives of the first, second, and third generations; both continue to live lives grounded in service to community.

“That’s where I had to sit when I got in trouble for talking too much!” says my mother, pointing at the ledge where she and her girlfriend sat giggling, punished by their teacher for their classroom disturbances. Eventually, both of my parents earned their teaching credentials at Fresno State—education, another inherited legacy.

Sometimes, my mother walked alone from the family farm to Grandview Elementary—days when her mother, a professional social worker, was working in the nearby town of Visalia, and her father was deep in the fields. She’d dive into the side ditch to avoid being sighted by oncoming cars, ashamed to be seen walking alone like that. Her father grew grapes; my mom and her two brothers were often left to their own devices, making their way through the ups and downs of ranch life. As we drive down Avenue 400, my mother points out the location of the surrounding family farms, many once owned by Japanese Americans: the Kawanos, the Nagatas, the Yamamotos, and so on—families who, I imagine, labored hard in the post-war years to rebuild their economies. Always, my mother’s two wishes were (1) to never marry a farmer and (2) to move to the city suburbs, both of which she accomplished.

We slowly approach the home on Jefferson Street where my father was raised, where his parents—Alma and Mitsuo—settled and lived following their release from the Gila River concentration camp. Grandpa worked for Otani’s market, a farming supply store; Grandma managed the home and children, worked in the local department store; everyone worked in the packing sheds in the summer. Neither of my Japanese American grandparents spoke much about their time in the camps or their reentry into civilian life; it’s taken me decades to understand the shape and nature of this silence. Many families lost everything—farms, homes, land, assets—and returned to communities that were, at best, indifferent to their reappearance. While driving by the Jefferson Street house, we glimpse the outline of the koi pond dug out in the front yard—commissioned by my grandfather. It looks just like the pond remnants my father and I witnessed at the Gila River camp this past summer: dusty, stone-specked ghosts from another era, signifying beauty, tradition, struggle—life.

Under a bright gray sky, we wander the Reedley Cemetery grounds on Reed Avenue, paying tribute to the dead, lingering at each marker for more storytalk. Three times more Korean immigrants and Korean Americans are buried in the Reedley Cemetery than in Dinuba’s Smith Mountain Cemetery, despite the fact that Dinuba had a much larger Korean community. This was, in part, due to Smith Mountain’s policy of segregating minorities into designated blocks, which discouraged burials there. My mother’s parents, Marilyn and Samuel, are buried beside their son, Timothy—my mother’s oldest brother, who was killed in a car accident at the age of twenty-five. “He died on Raisin Day,” she says, Dinuba’s annual harvest festival, September of 1976. “Raisin

Day didn't have the same meaning after my brother died." Nine months after that, my parents were married. "Life is short, we realized," says my mother. "Why don't we just get engaged now and get married? My Auntie Marie would always say: it's so good that you're getting married, your mom and dad are so happy, and it gives your mom something to focus on" (those months following Tim's passing). "Forty-two years later," says my mother, through tears. "Didn't work out so bad..."

Grandmother Alma Teranishi Saito (my father's mother) is also buried in the Reedley Cemetery, along with her parents and siblings. Her husband's—Mitsuo's—ashes were scattered by my father in the Sierras. Both of my parents have already secured their lots there, "overlooking the Kings River," says my mother. Three generations, one resting place.

Driving the South Valley streets, much has changed and much hasn't. Don's Shoes is still Don's Shoes; the site of the old library is now Rose Ann Vuich Park; Otani's market is now Valley Foods Supermarket, a *carniceria* and *taqueria*. I'm curious about life in Dinuba and Reedley in the present, so I ask a couple of friends and former students to share memories with me. "I loved to stop at Table Supply in downtown [Dinuba] and grab my monster energy drinks, and then go to Mega Video for a Frito boat and a *diablito*, which is shaved ice with chili, lime, and chamoy," says Aidan Castro. "It's really good. A lot of my memories are in the backyards of my friends' homes, but I would have to say Rose Ann Vuich Park was the place we went to the most. We would go there so often that whenever the *cholos* would show up to have a smoke session, they would just come up to us and greet us before they went their own way."

If you were to describe Reedley to someone not from California, how would you describe it? "If I had to tell them what Reedley is overall, I would say tradition," says Edgar Medina. "Reedley values tradition among many things as well as spirit. The people in Reedley work hard to make our name be known around the US, not just from school sports but also for the work we put in growing fruit for the world." "It's a beautiful place," says Alex Flores, of Dinuba. "The view of the Sierra Nevada mountains on a clear day is astounding. It used to be more common; every time the view is clear, people talk about how you used to be able to see it all the time."

On July 23, 1977, my parents were married at the Dinuba Presbyterian Church, with more than 300 people in attendance. A reception at the Dinuba Memorial Building on Alta Avenue followed. People—those who know the history of Japan's occupation of Korea—often ask me how my grandparents felt about my parents' relationship. No animosity reported, according to my folks—perhaps a testament to generational change, or a swiftly growing Asian America, or the card games hosted by each set of grandparents, where smoking and laughing and storytalking diffused any possibility of cultural tension.

Fresno was the big city my parents escaped to; the place where they met, in college, and made a home; the place from which my sister and I fled for even bigger cities;

S
R

the place I've returned to, decades later, to make life. "Dinuba feels so far away," my mother said once, despite the relatively short, straight-shot drive down the 99. But I think I'm beginning to understand what she meant. We grow far from the lands of our childhoods, expanding our inner and outer geographies with each day, place, and decade. We become doorways to memory, though so much lies dormant in us—each former self, sparked to life by a place's spirit, animated again by the scent of a riverbed, the sight of a winter orchard.

I love how my father eventually proposed to my mother—so much so, that his proposal made its way into a poem:

ACTS OF GRACE

Young in the Central Valley
recovering from football season
and summer fires, your mother
and father linger in the lot
outside his apartment.
"Maybe we should go
look at rings," says your father
and the river is set
the road unwinding.
In a small valley town
twenty miles east of here
your mother as a girl
cut grapes, braved spider fields
in the harvest heat.
Your father in the meantime
rumbled through boyhood
on the heels of war and his mother
and father's swift incarceration.
How is it they made their way
into each other's futures—
two tough, bright souls
enduring the crush of July
each in their own child ways?
They found each other.
They decided on each other
and a life with a garden
and two little girls practicing freedom
there in the walled space
with the jasmine and sparrows.

POSSIBLE FOOTSTEPS IN BERKELEY

ANNABELLE LONG

Start on Parker and Hillegass. Pull your right sock up; it's slipping and will be deeply uncomfortable in a block's time if you don't do something about it now. Adjust your mask and resent it for smelling like breath and detergent. Ignore the man yelling obscenities at you; he probably means you no harm, even if he sounds like he does. You can outrun him if he follows up on his threat to kill you anyways. Walk east.

Turn right on Benvenue. Walk south past the apartment where Patty Hearst was kidnapped and the gutters always stink of sewage and rotting leaves. Breathe through your mouth and examine the exterior for vulnerabilities, cracked windows or open doors where members of the Symbionese Liberation Army could have entered, cloaked in the darkness and chill of a February night in Berkeley. Perhaps they climbed in over the balcony. Wonder which unit was hers, how terrifying it must have been to be taken from it in the dead of night. Wonder who lives there now, if they know what their walls once witnessed.

Turn left on Derby. Bill Clinton and Hillary Rodham are reported to have spent the summer of 1971 in an apartment on your left. It seems hard to believe, them living in that drab, slightly decrepit building. It's somehow inspiring. They were probably in love then, pulsing with ambition and the spirit of centrism. Think about them taking their dirty sheets to the laundromat you'll pass when you turn right on College in a moment, a tangle of fabric and arms, quarters jangling in their pockets. What did they call the park down the road: Willard, for the suffragette, or Ho Chi Minh, as local anti-war activists did? How much was their rent?

Turn left on Forest and prepare yourself for the incline. The "old church" of St. John's Presbyterian is a block north and behind you on College, and its sanctuary since 1974 is on your right. The first pastor to lead the congregation in the old location was a casualty of the last Great American Pandemic, dying of influenza in 1918. The congregation was devastated and lost; let yourself feel their familiar sadness when you press your mask to your face and swing into the street to avoid coming within six feet of dog walkers and parents with strollers.

I call it, creatively, "The Route." There is a short version, and a long version, and neither existed before September in the year of the coronavirus. Physically, of course, they did, but not to me. My roommate went home for a week to focus on a paper about Nietzsche, and I found myself lonely and bored in our one-bedroom apartment, alternately reading books for classes and suppressing an upperclassman status-inspired anxiety about what I wanted to do with my life. My only answer to boredom seemed to be stomach-wrenching, tear-inducing rumination on the seemingly infinite yet ever-shrinking number of options available to me, and I needed a break from the apartment I semi-affectionately referred to as my "little box."

I couldn't turn to the ambient noise of a busy coffee shop, nor could I invite over a friend. Outside seemed to be my best—only—option. I'd mostly given up on the thrice-weekly 5Ks that I forced myself to run for two months during the summer; I'd grown tired of walking down Hillegass and Benvenue as far south as they'd take me after spending all of sophomore year making up excuses to walk the nearly three-mile round trip to Trader Joe's, and realized I'd never spent any time in the part of Berkeley bounded by College and Claremont Avenues.

And so I turned up on Forest one day, Garber the next, Stuart after that, and then Russell. According to data from my Fitbit, I walked for an average of an hour and a half every day that week. I followed dead ends to their conclusions, staircases to their bottoms, and accidentally, long driveways to their garages. I sweat into my mask, tried to think about nothing, and felt like I'd discovered something that was only mine.

☀ ☀ ☀

Continue all the way up Forest, past the house painted in blotchy yellows and oranges that looks like a big block of cheese, past the elementary school where you haven't seen any children in months. Don't think about it too much. At the top of the incline and near the end of the street, you'll pass through the brick and now-rusted iron gates to Claremont Court. The gates were erected in 1906 to attract professionals seeking privacy and wealthy neighbors. The center portions have since been removed so cars can drive through, but the feeling of exclusivity remains. Zillow will tell you that the cheapest home in the area is a cool $1.65 million, the most expensive a mind-numbing $4.91 million. Consider retaking the LSAT.

Turn right on Claremont Boulevard. Claremont runs into Monkey Island, a disappointing patch of shady, city-owned grass that has none of the monkeys its name suggests. The yellow municipal sign announcing the presence of a playground is laughably inaccurate. Off-duty San Francisco corporate lawyers and tech savants pick up after their purebred dogs, chatting about something probably much too expensive for you to eavesdrop on. There's always a girl reading on Monkey Island's solitary bench. Don't let it annoy you that she looks like a student, that she knows about your secret place and probably reads poetry or something else virtuous there while you stumble over your own worries and ambitions and shoelaces.

Continue south past the park and up Oak Knoll Terrace. Adjust your mask and pull your sock up in preparation for the final incline. The Oak Knoll houses are intimidating. They loom over the street, almost visibly passing judgment on people who walk by them and gawk at their grandeur. Covet them despite this. Imagine yourself reading in the sunny front room of your favorite dark brown house; think about drinking coffee on the gray house's balcony, watching the sun rise from behind the Claremont Hotel before zipping off to your important job in San Francisco. Know these fantasies are silly and trite but perhaps not entirely pointless, at least for the purpose of encouraging yourself to be optimistic about your future.

At the top of Oak Knoll, glance left towards the Claremont Hotel, but turn right on Avalon. The Claremont was here before many of these homes were; old photos show it sitting alone, a striking Tudor Revival tucked into the verdant, undeveloped hills of Berkeley. Its construction was interrupted by an earthquake in 1906, the thought of which underscores the precariousness of all of this. Your first home in Berkeley sat just feet from the Hayward Fault; you lived in a mouse-infested dorm room and with a low-simmering fear that, at any moment, the Earth might indulge its overdue desire to quake and swallow you whole. Do the people who live in Avalon's hilltop houses worry about them tumbling down, or is a century of relative geological stability enough reassurance?

Pause on the southern sidewalk before heading downhill. Look over the modern house's roof and through the trees toward the foggy blue of San Francisco. The view is ostensibly your reward for walking uphill, so savor it. Think about driving on city streets you can't see from here, how many people you're looking at. Are there people in those office buildings right now? Are they looking back?

☀ ☀ ☀

When I was little, one of my favorite toys was a talking globe. It was shiny and plastic and came with a stylus I could use to press on any country I wanted to and find out something interesting about it.

"Where are the Falkland Islands? Andorra? Uzbekistan?" my parents would quiz me, and I'd dutifully spin the globe and point to each of them, eager for my next command. This made me no friends in preschool, and I've since forgotten all of the geographical trivia I knew as a four-year-old, but I've never quite shaken my interest in places and their histories. After weeks spent circling the same blocks and admiring the same houses, I naturally felt an urgent need to figure out what I was actually looking at.

☀ ☀ ☀

Proceed down Avalon. Halfway down, Pine Path is on your left. It's one of the 137 man-made paths running through the hills of Berkeley, serving as shortcuts for quick navigation of the city and emergency exits in case of a fire or an earthquake or both. From the top of the staircase, you have an excellent view of Claremont's treetops, the fluffy rounds of leaves that form canopies over streets in the summer and clog gutters in the fall. At the bottom of Avalon Avenue, turn onto Avalon Walk, another veiny little path. It spits you out onto Palm Court, which turns into Stuart Street after a few steps. Stuart was once the northern border of Kelsey Ranch, where the elms grew that gave Elmwood its name.

Turn left on Kelsey Street. Some of these trees must be nineteenth-century elms. Try to remember what an elm looks like and turn right on Russell. Walk west for five blocks, across Piedmont and Cherry and College and Benvenue, all the way to Hillegass. Turn right. All of this land used to be the Hillegass Tract and, despite its proximity to campus, was originally developed for spacious houses intended for families and professionals—a downhill, downscale version of the luxury of Claremont Court. Many of the structures are now duplexes or crowded communal homes, consequences of the Bay Area's depressingly expensive housing market. Look at the brown-shingled house on the corner of Hillegass and Russell with all its eaves and awnings and balconies presumably attached to cozy attic bedrooms. Reflect on the thing you seem to have for dark brown houses. For big houses, expensive houses. Is it optimism or delusion to imagine yourself living there? Are those even that different?

Walk north past Willard Park and across Derby. Before Derby Street was Derby Street, it was Derby Creek, a life-giving stream of water that flowed from the hills to the edge of the bay. An important Ohlone village, marked by the presence

of a shellmound, sat at the mouth of it in what's now Emeryville. The earliest outside settlers built their homes along creeks, which they eventually paved over and largely erased from maps. On rainy days, the creeks try to make themselves known again, pushing up through storm drains and flooding thirsty non-native lawns, but for most of the year, they exist in darkness, underground and ignored. The street in front of your apartment turns into something resembling a river when it rains for more than a day; is it willing itself to be a creek again? The characteristic impermanence of college town life seems a bit deceptive in light of this.

Turn left on Parker. UC Berkeley's youngest professor lived around the corner from here, on Regent, in the late '60s before retreating to rural Montana to live without running water or electricity and send bombs in the mail. He probably hated Willard Park; he certainly hated Berkeley. Who lives in his old backyard cottage now; do they know the Unabomber once slept and ate and lived where they do? Is that a selling point for the landlord?

* * *

I often think in anachronisms, layering visions of the past onto scenes from my present. The Unabomber fuses with the men who enthusiastically make catcalls at me from bus stops and moving cars, even though I know his hatred for women and technology were generally expressed privately or with actual explosives. The young Bill and Hillary sit amongst the impossibly well-postured picnickers in Willard Park, even though they probably spent most of their time indoors, poring over legal briefs for their internships. I think about myself as a future resident of Claremont Court, even though none of my interests are particularly lucrative.

I like to imagine myself as someone just passing through, a footprint in the sand. Somehow existing in a time that is uniquely mine but also with everyone and everything who has ever existed here alongside me.

* * *

The Route ends at the 2500 block of Parker Street, where you started. The historical record reveals nothing notable about your apartment complex, no famous former residents or exciting and horrible crimes, though you know hundreds of people have lived here before. In 1961, the year folk singer Malvina Reynolds turned 61, she found Parker Street to be a suitable subject of a song. "I'd rather go to the corner store / Than sing hosanna on that golden shore," she crooned in "This World," probably before the corner store was a 7-Eleven. "I'd rather live on Parker Street / Than fly around where the angels meet," the "Muse of Parker Street" continued. A fitting ode to the quotidian beauty of the street, to the people who exist beyond the pages of recorded history.

Try to understand her love for Parker Street as you enter your apartment to catch the last minutes of the sunset through the front window. Kick your shoes off at the door and peel off your terrible socks. Remove your mask and wipe your face without feeling too disgusted at how damp it is.

Look out the window but also around the room. Golden light pushes past the tangle of telephone lines and tree branches outside and makes its way onto your living room wall as if on display, a brief but striking moment that seems to greet the impending darkness kindly. That same light reaches the hills to the east, and the houses packed together are for a moment hued with rose, warm and breathing and full of life, gulping in the last bits of sunlight before the evening's arrival. To the west, gaps between rooftops and treetops and phone lines reveal pieces of San Francisco: Sutro Tower standing tall and alone, buildings stacked side by side, and the milky blue of the Bay at the foot of the headlands to the north. Downtown Oakland reveals itself similarly to the south, squat buildings poking up through the trees and into the light. Through the bedroom window and to the north is the Campanile, a reminder of why this apartment is lived in at all. Malvina must have been thinking about this time of day when she wrote that song.

☀ ☀ ☀

The 2500 block of Parker Street is three miles from the easternmost house visible from my front window, and three miles from the eastern edge of the Bay. It's four miles from downtown Oakland, and two miles from north Berkeley.

The 2500 block of Parker Street is in the heart of South Berkeley, which feels like the center of the world. My world, at least. Its position makes it a curious place to be twenty years old, to become myself. Walking along The Route, intended to be a head-clearing endeavor, only fills it with more possibilities, more ideas, more questions, for it seems that every possible life trajectory exists within several blocks of my bedroom. To be the future First Couple or their leftist neighbors; to be a Claremont Court resident or a person sleeping at the foot of their hills; to be an invisible person in a skyscraper or a person squinting to see them; to be a leaf in a canopy or a leaf in a gutter; to be a fault line or house built on top of it; to be a 150-year-old elm or a creek forced underground; to be 2808 Oak Knoll Terrace or 2500 Parker Street.

It's not that it all seems possible—I know I will never become the Unabomber or Patty Hearst—but that it's all here, together, existing in common and in contradiction. The cliché goes that history repeats itself, but it feels more accurate to say that history overlaps with itself, that it builds on top of itself and erases itself and reveals itself again. In "This World," Malvina Reynolds gets at this feeling: "Somebody else will take my place / Some other hands, some other face / Some other eyes will look around / And find the things I've never found." I like to think of myself as the somebody else.

FRED'S GOIN' TO CALIFORNIA

FRED WILLIAMS WITH SUE MARK AND HEIDI HERRERA

If you live in the East Bay and travel the busy San Pablo Avenue corridor, you've likely passed Williams Appliances. The squat maroon wooden building, a reminder of the area's nineteenth-century agricultural past, straddles North Oakland, Southwest Berkeley, and Emeryville.

Since the 1980s, Fred Williams has been tirelessly working at Williams Appliances, one of the few remaining Black-owned legacy businesses in North Oakland. Fred is part of a disappearing generation of history keepers interviewed by Sue Mark, cultural researcher, North Oakland neighbor, and initiator of local history project Commons Archive. Fred's story echoes that of many North Oakland Black families: their arrival from the South, their cultivation of community support to counter disinvestment and structural violence, and for many, their exodus. Even as new developments populate the neighborhood, Fred keeps his doors open to the community he is committed to sustaining.

In these interview excerpts, condensed and lightly edited for clarity, Fred Williams talks about his migration from Alabama, the Black neighborhood culture he encountered in North Oakland, and the consequences of its subsequent disappearance. Fred no longer lives in this neighborhood. But the community-oriented work ethic he inherited from his uncle along with the family business drives his determination to stay.

FRED: Pop used to tell me, 'You got to be here every day.' He was committed—you got to keep the doors open. I mean, they saw [his] old red pickup truck every day—people look to see the person who's runnin' the place. If he's excited about the place, people come in—the gift that we give them is good customer service.

Since the 1960s, Williams Appliances has furnished rentals in the surrounding neighborhood with high-quality, affordable, used appliances. Fred doesn't just sell fridges and stoves. He's invested in building long-term neighborhood relationships, something nearby profit-driven, big-box retailers can never do. A purchase at Fred's shop includes entry into his supportive network.

FRED: For Pop, it was a meeting ground. We would sit out there, and we would have friends on top of friends—they would come here, and they would be talkin' for hours.

People was here all day. Those were great days.

Known affectionately as "Pop," Benjamin Williams was Fred's father figure and mentor. He was part of the Second Great Migration (starting in the 1940s), when many Black people from the South settled in Oakland as wartime workers. Determined to be his own boss after working at a furniture store, Benjamin Williams started his own shop. He intuitively knew that his style of business smarts would also nurture community.

FRED: Pop used to tell me, you can't be Black in business and beat people out their money; you ain't gonna last. He believed that if you buy your stuff here, he wanted you to come back.

Fred's a busy man, but he always takes his time with passersby: a wave, a clap on the back, a short conversation. Part of his rural Alabama roots, his kindness has never eroded even after over three decades of living in Oakland. Williams Appliances is a place where people know they are welcome to visit, catch up, meet others, and learn neighborhood news.

FRED: We have good days, and we have bad days just like any other business. But the doors are still open. The community, yes, it is changed. But as you noticed, you could sit out there with me, and I speak to everybody. See, that's part of community, too.

☀ ☀ ☀

FRED: In Alabama, we got a million trees. The first thing I noticed about being here is it smelled horrible. We grew up poor—but we still didn't want for anything. We ate off the land. My goodness. We ate good. We had family. Family was tight.

Stories flow from trust. It took many visits to Fred's shop before he shared his painful childhood history, how Jim Crow pushed him from his home and the family that he loved.

FRED: There was nothing there for me in Alabama, baby. It was all over for me. I had been accused of a drawing that I didn't commit. You know, back in them days a little cartoon, that I had got accused by one of the teachers of doin'—in them days racism was hot. I mean, you just didn't cross the line. So when I left, it was the toughest thing I had to do—really it was. I can't even express the feeling, going to a whole other world, another planet.

Originating as an Ohlone trail, San Pablo Avenue spans twenty-three miles of East Bay communities and is part of the oldest continuously used route in the US. Waves of transit evolution, from horse and buggy to streetcar and bus, have impacted the way people use

WILLIAMS APPLIANCES

and experience individual districts along the avenue. Contemporary car culture further erodes social connections and discourages impromptu interactions, which are fundamental to cultivating a sense of place.

FRED: San Pablo, oh my goodness. I was walking across the street like a little child holding hands—looking both ways because I wasn't used to the cars. I wasn't used to the size of the street. I wasn't used to the amount of people that I saw. It was a total culture shock.

Williams Appliances, as a business that prioritizes relationships over transactions, maintains neighborhood belonging. When Fred arrived in the 1980s, this once stable area was ravaged by the crack epidemic. Movie theaters, department stores, bars, clubs, restaurants, and groceries—at their peak in the 1960s—were all but gone by the 1990s. New freeways, eminent domain, and unequal municipal investment made this area a no-man's-land.

FRED: You have to understand, this area didn't look like [it does now]. It was really run down. We had prostitutes all up and down the street. Drugs was everywhere...and a lot of people got hurt. In those days, it was just a tough area. When I first got out here, you call the police, you'd be waiting for days. They ain't comin'. Callin' the police now, they'll be right here.

Since the 1940s, Black migrants from the South, like Benjamin Williams, circumnavigated decades of redlining in Oakland. They bought residential properties in pockets throughout North and West Oakland. Old Victorians were converted into duplexes and triplexes; landlords were neighbors. Block clubs and mutual support flourished. Folks left their front doors unlocked and shared backyard fruit harvested from trees planted by Italian and Portuguese predecessors. Fred experienced only traces of this era.

FRED: There was a few other older businesses that was here. At that time, there was really nothing but Black people around here. People had been in the community for years up and down here.

People didn't have money. Even in those days, fifty dollars for a washing machine, wow. Pop would hire people off the street to come and go with me to just make a couple of dollars to take the deliveries—it was a self-run business.

Fred met his wife Ruthanne on one of these deliveries, installing a fridge in her family's home. On one of their first dates, his friendly practice of waving to everyone worried her as the pair drove around Oakland. She thought it would get him in trouble. Undaunted, Fred said it's just what you do.

Williams Appliances provided more than much-needed affordable appliances. Pop created a place where community could gather, a place of his own where he loved to be. This informal hub cultivated safety, especially for Black elders. It also provided a safe harbor for Fred when he needed it most. A fatal car accident left Fred fatherless as a young boy. At eighteen, Fred left Alabama for California. He settled under his uncle's wing, staying there until his uncle's passing in 2012.

FRED: Pop was determined to be self-employed, and not have to ask anybody for anything. And it ended up being that way. I miss him, oh my God. I miss him so much. We talked almost every day. Me and him had a real tight bond. Seventy-six years old—in this day and time, to me, it's a little bit too young to leave this earth.

FRED: Everybody's saying the same thing about this neighborhood—it's pushing the poor out and the people that can't pay. The culture of Black people that used to be here, that's gone altogether.

Foreclosures, soaring home prices, and rent increases are now pricing out long-time residents. As Black elders pass, extended families cash out inherited properties to predatory "flippers." From Fred's perspective, this unsustainable neighborhood evolution, combined with rapid development, amounts to mass displacement. Known as the birthplace of the Black Panthers and now home to Pixar and biotech industries, this area used to be economically and culturally diverse.

FRED: When I first got here, there was nothing but Black people. I mean, all day long, Black people, they're everywhere. Nowadays I can sit out there and I may see one or two a day.

In 2010, Black neighbors were just under half of North Oakland's population; eight years later, only a quarter of residents were Black. Today, the numbers are even lower. A comparison of 2010 and 2020 US Census data reveals that for every four days in the last ten years, one Black person disappeared from North Oakland neighborhoods.

FRED: This neighborhood is changing. In the next five years, there won't be no more Blacks around here, no more families. People and investors putting up all these multiplex units that you and I can't afford. It will be just the twenty-five to thirty-five age group in this area.

Fred's small but mighty shop is overshadowed by several new multistory apartments that are inaccessible to longtime neighbors rooted in the community for generations. People move in, stay for shorter periods, and are less connected to the community. Realtors, by rebranding the area with a new name, have attempted to erase the neighborhood's history. Newcomers have little incentive to learn about local culture.

FRED: The wind don't even blow here no more the same since they put these big ol' buildings up. It's colder across the street over there, when it used to be nice and warm. Most people in the building over there now, they ain't gonna talk to you. They in and out. So the bond of the community is changing.

Places that once nurtured connections, like Williams Appliances, are disappearing. Fred laments how new housing developments have dramatically shifted the Golden Gate neighborhood from its Black working-class roots. These demographic changes translate into a rapid loss of decades-old neighborhood networks. According to Pop, consistent visual presence was the best way to attract business. Until recently, Fred and his crew would pull out their wares every morning—refurbished washers, fridges, stoves—to hug the shop's corner.

FRED: If you saw twenty, thirty appliances out there every day, that alone let people know we're here. Now, because the city tells me somebody is complaining, we can't do that. I can't put nothing out there without them tell[ing] me I am breaking the law. So yes, the change is affecting business. Yes, we've seen a cut in customers. Yes, people driving down the street thinkin' we done closed now because they don't see all the appliances out there and even when I would put just a few out front, they became a 'blight, an eyesore.'

If his wares can't announce Williams Appliances, at least the building's distinctive signage might. Unequal investment from the City of Oakland has harmed Fred's livelihood. By prioritizing the complaints of new neighbors, the city has destabilized one of the neighborhood's anchor businesses.

FRED: I got a tree right out there. I done called [the city] a hundred times. 'Y'all come trim the tree, man. Can't even see the shop.' They tell me they ain't got no budget. But right next door to that high-rise building there was a city truck trimming the tree. And I go up and tell them 'Hey, man, can y'all come trim the tree.' And they say they can't, it ain't on the schedule. And I can't touch that tree. That's City property. And right there it is growing up all over the place, and nobody won't do nothin' about it.

As the appliance industry changes, Fred continues to pivot to keep his business healthy and relevant. No longer made to last, refurbished fridges and washers now cost more than they can be sold for. In response, Fred is implementing a business model with both cultural and environmental sustainability at its core.

FRED: Appliances that we're buying in stores today are crap; they're not made to last anymore. Recycling is the key. We recycle everything now. I recycle plastic, doors, cords, everything. There are so many appliances out there—they need to be recycled.

While many of the new neighbors in the surrounding high-rises look for ways to lessen their carbon footprint, whether through using reusable shopping bags or eating less meat, their dismissal of Williams Appliances as a blight ignores a crucial component of sustainability—meaningful connections with one another.

Fred keeps the doors of Williams Appliances open, not because he has to, but because he wants to. For Fred, the continuity of his family's business isn't about making a profit. Fred Williams is not only a businessman, he is a soul keeper. Williams Appliances is part of an extended neighborhood family. Knowing Fred's story keeps this legacy alive.

☀ ☀ ☀

Fred's story is now archived in a new neighborhood reference collection at the Oakland Public Library's Golden Gate Branch. For Ruthanne, Fred's wife, "This book is healing, it is a gift. To think that Fred's children and grandchildren will read his stories, printed in these books…we never dreamed of this happening."

Fred stays because he cares about cultural sustainability and maintaining relationships in this community. Honoring Fred's experience and wisdom, and that of other longtime North Oakland Black neighbors, ensures that local public knowledge reflects the community's diversity and complexity. Living in the same place doesn't mean we know how to live together.

FRED: I want to keep this going because my uncle had enough faith in me to believe that I would do whatever I could to keep this door up. He loved this business. This was his baby. And I love it, too.

GOOD VIBRATIONS FROM CALIFORNIA'S DEAF GEOGRAPHIES

PETER SEBASTIAN CHESNEY

There is something missing from the geographies and histories of California. A clue to the lost opportunities for a Deaf California dates to 1896, when an Iowa man wrote a letter quoted in the *San Francisco Call* to the Asylum for the Deaf and Dumb in Berkeley. Administrators forwarded the message to the state's trade office, which extended a warm invitation to several Deaf farmers hoping to found a colony, "near a running stream...and on a soil specifically adapted to the raising of corn."

The letter writer, John J. Thompson of Corning, was not able to hear, nor could he speak, but he wrote as an advocate for numerous other "deaf-mutes" in the area. Thompson was in his late forties when California learned of him and his "silent community." By 1900, Thompson was still in Iowa, according to the US Census, and the enumerator acknowledged John and his wife Alice's deafness by writing a simple "No" in the column labeled "Can Speak English." A component intended to collect data about recalcitrant non-English speakers, often immigrants, had netted two proud Deaf separatists. (Please take note how I capitalize "Deaf" when referencing a culture or members of a people, but then switch to lowercase, person-first language regarding the physiological condition of deafness.)

California has rarely heard of itself as a Deaf magnet, and Deaf people—or Half Deaf people like me—often balk at such phrasing in social scientific projects to fill the gap. Can Deaf people speak? Listen closely to the archive! Blah. Requiring Deaf people to use voices—rarely ours—to ease your comprehension evokes the oralist and assimilative process known in the nineteenth century as "articulation." Educators used to force Deaf people to form their breath into sounds they could not hear and to read the speaking lips of other people to make life simpler for hearing majorities. The one-sided toll of this process was the last thing many in the Deaf minority wanted. Plenty of people who live with deafness now still don't want anything along these lines. Instead, we demand new theoretical frameworks that include Deaf imaginaries without requiring Deaf peoples of past, present, or future to play a part to which the normative "hearing" subject can relate.

With this in mind, I speculate about the factors pushing a community of Deaf Iowans to consider exile to another state. An easterly wind of ableist thought was blowing. Alexander Graham Bell, the telephone inventor, robber baron, and self-appointed anti-Deaf activist, marked all Deaf colonies and institutions for dissolution, urged all Deaf people to disperse, and hoped for all Deaf culture to fade away. His 1885 speech listing these recommendations was reprinted so widely that it was featured in San Francisco's *Daily Alta California*. Bell's central rationalization for keeping people with deafness away from one another was boldly eugenicist. He opposed the marriage of two persons with deafness for fear this physiological trait would pass to the next generation. A leading scientist of the era, Bell helped establish a scholarly discourse in support of "purging the race of its degenerate qualities" through the elimination of Deaf people. By the way, the Thompsons had five children, none of whom experienced deafness, but even if they had...

Deaf people in California defied the bigotry of Bell and found one another. In 1901, W.C. Ullrich heralded "the Los Angeles Association of the Deaf" in the *Los Angeles Herald*. The paper, oriented to workers as opposed to the bourgeois *Los Angeles Times*, listed members of this club by name and occupation. "Tilley" clerked on the postal route to San Francisco. Norman Lewis managed a print shop. Leo Williams won a contract to install sewers in Santa Ana. Institutions serving Deaf people included St. Paul's, the church that hosted the association's meetings, and the Spring Street School, where students came to learn "the oral method." Mrs. Bennett and Taylor were trained to teach a multimodal mix of sign language and rote articulation. Graduates presumably went into careers as carpenters and electricians, cigar makers, and gravediggers. However, the Association wanted more potential for upward social mobility. The state's only Deaf high school, that "Asylum," was too far to the north. Deaf community leaders believed enough children with deafness lived in Southern California for a campus closer to Los Angeles.

In Porterville, 1912, Deaf people proceeded to found a colony of their own. Twenty-five "mutes" named themselves the Cogswell Club after Alice Cogswell. The *Chico Record* reported this iconic young woman, who had died aged twenty-five in 1830, had been "the first teacher of manual language in America." The imprint of a Deaf perspective marked this comment, for Cogswell had been noteworthy in the first years of American Sign Language. The nine-year-old girl modeled her "manualist" capacity to sign in view of Reverend Thomas H. Gallaudet, a fully hearing adult tutor who went on to observe various Europeans speaking with their hands. In the East, Gallaudet's memory endured as a teacher of sign, a founder of a Deaf school in Hartford, and the father of the founder of Washington, DC's Gallaudet University. Deaf pride sidelined the Gallaudet family legacy in favor of Cogswell. However, this group still propagated an ableism of its own. The club condemned "beggars" feigning deafness. Readers were asked to dismiss any such person seeking charity as an imposter because Deaf communities universally cared for their own. The club offered to help investigate any malingerers and elaborated in a 1915 issue of the *Madera Mercury*: "No real deaf mute ever begs. He is capable of earning his own living."

California was indeed a land of opportunity for Deaf people who earned a living by participating in a cultural renaissance. Granville Redmond, a painter and performer who was unable to hear since his childhood in the 1870s, offered a case study in Deaf expression. His landscape portraits testified to the centrality of visualism in the modernity project, which included Deaf claims to an authoritative position as masterful at seeing. Titles like *Quiet Moonlight*, *Talk on the Beach*, and *The Mowers (When Hearts Beat as One)* asserted a special Deaf way of knowing quiet, conversation, and limbic resonance. Meanwhile, hearing subjects likely assumed such notions were essentially foreign to people with deafness. Redmond also adroitly stepped into silent filmmaking with Charlie Chaplin, a vaudevillian child actor who knew how to eschew mouthing words in favor of theatrical communicative gesture and dynamic facial expressions. In several films, Granville used sign language on the screen to communicate with Chaplin. To hire Deaf performers mattered at a time when oralist administrators had dismissed many manualist Deaf professionals from Deaf institutions. This cinematic moment was like a golden age for Deaf filmgoers. According to Deaf historian John S. Schuchman, they went to cinemas and enjoyed the same films made for any given hearing person, until the tragedy of the talkies.

After World War II, when Deaf workers had received public recognition for working diligently as quality inspectors in munitions factories, California earmarked funds for a second school for children with deafness. A 1946 press release in the *Los Angeles Times* announced the search for a site for this facility and then mentioned the state had already selected Atascadero for its new maximum security facility for caging the criminally insane and Riverside County for "either a prison or hospital." That the state turned attention to penal, medical, and educational institutions all at the same time was no coincidence. A prison called California Institution for Women (CIW) opened in Corona in 1952. The next year, California School for the Deaf at Riverside (CSDR) opened less than twenty miles to CIW's east. A 1954 photograph in the *Los Angeles Examiner*, archived digitally at the Los Angeles Public Library, illustrated the significance of this proximity. Pictured were busy CIW inmates, workers whose task was to do 30,000 pounds of laundry per week for the prison staff members and for their families. That total weight rose by 20,000 a week because prison workers assumed the burden of laundry trucked in from the CSDR boarding school residents while classes were in session. The state had rendered disabled and criminalized citizens interdependent. Captive workers at the prison did cheap labor in service for Deaf students. As recently as the year 2000, CIW inmates caged in the "golden gulag," per Ruth Wilson Gilmore, still occupied a similar role. Some were reading aloud and recording audio versions of school textbooks for students with blindness and dyslexia.

Standing with backs turned in that *Los Angeles Examiner* photograph were captive workers, and many readers of the time would have noticed a couple of these women were Black. This is no reason to pit the categories of racism and ableism against one another. The violence of the administrative state, not Deaf people, forced these Black women to serve children with disabilities. Like Robert McGruer, Jasbir Puar, and theorists in DisCrit (critical disability theory), I recognize how debility intersects with life in communities of color. The children of working-class Black families are more likely to become blind, deaf, or mobility-impaired due to unequal access to medical care and uneven distributions of violence. Police have a history of liberally using "the right to maim" against Black men and boys. Long-term health effects of such debilitating shootings are referenced in the name for the "Crips" gang.

In the summer of 2020, some Black Lives Matter protesters showed up for racial justice carrying signs reading, "All Black Lives Matter," "Trans Black Lives Matter," and "Deaf Black Lives Matter." This last message in particular jarred me as a white person with single-sided hearing. I took another look at my notes, and suddenly I found a new framework for the shooting of a middle-aged motorist named John Grudt. In the winter of 1965, LAPD stalked Grudt through the nighttime streets of South Los Angeles. From an unmarked car, they shouted at the motorist to stop. When Grudt did not react, the cops broadcast a radio message to an officer in plainclothes waiting by the next intersection. He approached Grudt's car and tapped the window with the muzzle of a shotgun. Grudt tried to speed off from the potential assailant, but he was shot dead. The family later testified that Grudt was "hard of hearing," according to the historian Max Felker-Kantor. Since I have had total deafness in my left ear for a decade, I can state with authority how easy it is to miss instructions from authorities and how jarring it is to have a person jump into my left-side field of vision. Many of us who experience deafness or single-sided hearing loss reside in California, so there you have one more good reason to disarm police. Officers with guns are a far greater risk to us than they are to hearing people. The multiple marginalities of deafness in an ableist society compounded with racialization mark Black, Brown, and Indigenous Deaf lives for an unusually high likelihood of death by cop.

Grudt was not the only Deaf person who found his way into my research. Another was Brian Wilson of The Beach Boys. My research impressionistically reads sensory experiences in the postwar car culture as articulations of belonging to a gender, a race, a sexuality, or a nationality in Southern California. All four categories intersected advantageously to empower Brian, a man who was white, straight, and raised in suburban Hawthorne. Additionally, he was deaf in one ear. In a 2016 memoir, the rock star introduced his father as a working man who had lost an eye to a workplace injury. Often pulling the glass eye out and making the boys look into the socket as a punishment, this grown man also beat them severely enough to deafen Brian. Nevertheless, Brian sang with his brothers and began writing original lyrics for sunshine pop songs. The work of Phil Spector, an innovator in the studio production of monaural sound, resonated with Brian. Just as Deaf culture valued silent films, this music recorded in "mono" has a special appeal to Half Deaf listeners who cannot hear "stereo." The 1966 hit "Good Vibrations" by The Beach Boys remains, to my one ear, an anthem from California's history and geography for those of us dreaming of a Half Deaf culture of our own.

ACKNOWLEDGMENTS

We're forever grateful to California's writers, artists, activists, and cultural institutions who help us understand its past and to see it anew. Our time as editors at KCET, *Tropics of Meta*, *Boom California*, and *Huizache* have broadened our intellectual community, provided us a space to think about craft and place, and encouraged us to swim across genres. We thank our former and current colleagues at these publications. Big thanks to Jason Sexton for entrusting us with *Boom California*, and to Ofelia Cuevas for carrying the torch.

Finding a home isn't always easy and we are grateful to Angel City Press for their immediate enthusiasm, expert care, and attention. Like all their books, this one is a beautiful object. Special shout out to Terri Accomazzo.

Fresno State and Claremont Graduate University housed *Boom California* from 2018–2020, and 2020–2021, respectively. We thank them for their institutional support.

Above all, we thank our families who continue to support us, inspire us, and take part in our journeys.

— Carribean Fragoza, Romeo Guzmán, and Samine Joudat

ABOUT THE EDITORS

CARRIBEAN FRAGOZA

Carribean Fragoza was named after a body of water. Though she is a terrible swimmer, she insists on living as close as possible to three bodies of water: the Pacific Ocean, the San Gabriel River, and Legg Lake. Ironies abound. The San Gabriel Valley will forever be her home but wherever she goes, she needs at least one mountain to orient her. She is interested in the inner lives of rocks, plants, and birds. If she had unlimited wealth and influence, she would channel all of it to empowering Indigenous people to recover their homeland and their ancestral knowledge of all nature.

ROMEO GUZMÁN

Romeo Guzmán was born in Goleta, California to migrant parents from Guadalajara; he has deep affinities for Pomona and South El Monte/El Monte. He came to know Pomona by practicing and playing at many of its elementary, middle school, and high schools *futbol* fields. He hung out at the old pool hall on second street, where the owner, Leo, played classic rock. He has come to know El Monte and South El Monte through family parties and celebrations as well as the slow and beautiful labor of collaboratively writing its history. To learn more visit romeoguzman.com

SAMINE JOUDAT

The movement that has shaped Samine Joudat's upbringing in the world—born in Iran before immigrating to different parts of the United States and Europe via Ecuador—now shapes the way he thinks of home. Beyond a place locked into land, he finds home in moments, people, notes, and words, too. His mind is never far from pondering the forces that uproot, displace, and transfigure notions of home and the longing we often feel for it. He finds duty, meaning, and joy in the negotiation between looking back in search of recovery and looking forward in search of transformation. He hopes that all beings are afforded the dignity to do the same. Find him on Instagram @saminejoudat.

ABOUT THE CONTRIBUTORS

JENNIFER CARR

Neither of Jennifer Carr's US-born grandfathers spoke English first—totally normal in San Pedro, where someone can grab coffee and still hear Croatian, Italian, Korean, Spanish, and Japanese from people who consider themselves collectively San Pedran. She is a born/raised/returned San Pedran, where the Carrs emigrated in the 1910s and the Perezes around 1900. (Thanks most likely to an Italian majority used to the saint's name as Pietro, the town's name has morphed unequivocally to the hybrid PEE-dro. Please don't say PAY-dro. That's someplace else.) San PEEdrans' collective DNA means everyone's related to a dockworker and (often unfortunately) knows everyone else's business.

WENDY CHENG

Wendy Cheng was born in Madison, Wisconsin to parents who came as student migrants from Taiwan. After her father was blacklisted from returning to Taiwan for his political activism, her parents moved the family to San Diego. However, it wasn't until after she left Southern California as a young adult that she realized it was home. After living in Massachusetts, New York, the Bay Area, and Arizona, she went home. Now she lives in Pasadena, where she looks at the San Gabriel Mountains every day and contemplates the more-than-human world as much as she can. For more, go to wendycheng.com.

PETER SEBASTIAN CHESNEY

Peter Sebastian Chesney is Californian. He was born there, though that hardly makes a Californian. He became Californian as he studied California history at UCLA, as he worked T.A. jobs for a state paycheck, and as he served as a steward in UAW 2865. He became Californian as he wrote public policy histories that built momentum in Sacramento for statewide rent controls and the abolition of R-1 zoning. He became Californian as he was priced out of L.A., as he raised a baby with his partner in a 600-square-foot mountain cottage, and as he qualified for Medi-Cal.

FERNANDO CORONA

Fernando Corona was born and raised in Mexicali. Since he was a kid, he has traveled across the border as if it didn't exist. For a short period, he lived in Seattle where he started doing art, but the weather took him back to Mexicali; like the migrant birds, he missed the sun. He has always enjoyed painting (canvas and murals alike) and draws inspiration from all Californian punk-skate-hiphop-*Norteño* scenes of the '90s as well as the DIY education he acquired at Mexicali Rose. Now he is trying to become one good ol' desert wizard. For more, follow him on Instagram @fernandomendezcorona.

LISA COVERT

Lisa Covert was born and raised in the Antelope Valley, California's high desert. Her parents also grew up in the AV, although like most people there, they came from somewhere else. As a child she mostly looked forward to leaving the desert. She finally left to attend college in Long Beach, and after that, made her way east to Connecticut and South Carolina. But she's still a Californian at heart. Her family keeps drawing her back to the desert, and she now has a greater appreciation for the vast arid landscape, especially after living in the humidity of Charleston.

ELAINE LEWINNEK

When the American Studies department at California State University Fullerton interviewed Elaine Lewinnek for a job, nineteen years ago, she had to check a map to find where Fullerton was. Since then, she continues to try to understand where she is, learning from students, colleagues, family, neighbors, archives, walking, biking her kids to school, and especially lately from her co-authors of *A People's Guide to Orange County*, Gustavo Arellano and Thuy Vo Dang.

RAMÓN GARCÍA

Ramón García was an undocumented child, although his parents had legally immigrated to Modesto, California from Michoacán, Mexico, when he was six years old. He grew up in Modesto when it was culturally removed from the Bay Area. As far as he knows, in high school, he was the only Mexican/Chicano teenager in Modesto who was a fan of the Smiths. Later, when he came to Los Angeles during his college years at UC Santa Cruz, he found out that the Smiths had a significant Chicanx following in LA. That's when he realized that art and identity are not geographically fixed, but perhaps are a translation, adaptation and transformation of chosen cultures. ramongarciaphd.com

CHRIS GREENSPON

Chris Greenspon's Tinder bio used to read "#1 in the SGV." Now he's married to a woman from Baldwin Park. A few years ago, during one of his various "funemployment" stints from his spotty radio career, he stumbled onto the idea of making short form documentaries (or long form radio features) about the San Gabriel Valley. He, of halfie-suburban-La Puente-Covina stock, realized there was something invaluable about helping others express their connection to home, especially in an overlooked place. Doing this helped him grapple with his own identity—as a podcaster—and *SGV Weekly* was born.

RUXANDRA GUIDI

Ruxandra (Rux) Guidi grew up far from California, in Caracas, Venezuela, a few minutes from El Ávila National Park and a short drive from the Caribbean Sea. As a teenager, she migrated to the US and eventually found her way to Berkeley in her mid-twenties. Her journalism would take her across the state, from rural communities to rural areas, from forests to deserts. But the Eastern Coachella Valley, with its tight knit farm working communities and long history of environmental injustices, kept drawing her back like no other place. Today, she lives in the adjacent Sonoran Desert of Tucson, Arizona.

MYRIAM GURBA

Myriam Gurba was born in the windy Santa Maria Valley, a region celebrated for its strawberry fields, wineries, and tri tip barbecue. She loves the entire Golden State and can prove it: she has lived in Northern, Central, and Southern California. She currently lives in a sunny bungalow surrounded by native plants and palm trees. Two of her grandparents are buried in California cemeteries, and she hopes to join them someday. That way, she'll really become part of this place.

DAVID HELPS

Born on the territory of the Haudenosaunee, David Helps grew up in a small town in Ontario, Canada, that lies—like much of California—between breadbasket and rust belt. David came to writing about LA by way of living in Toronto, a city almost as convinced of its own exceptionalism but with worse weather. He currently organizes with the Graduate Employees Organization, Local 3550 of the American Federation of Teachers, and gets homesick more often than he admits. More of his work can be found at david-helps.com.

HEIDI HERRERA

Raised in rural San Diego, Heidi Herrera is a cultural worker with a deep respect for land and its stewards. As a new neighbor in Oakland, Heidi learned lifelong lessons in tending to community from long-time residents. Now in Los Angeles, Heidi shares historically marginalized artists' stories from California and beyond.

MELISSA MORA HIDALGO

The doctor had to use forceps to bring Melissa Mora Hidalgo into this world at Beverly Hospital in Montebello that Tuesday afternoon in February, 1974. Her mom said she was born looking like she'd been in an alley fight, an apt description for a baby girl who would grow up and have to fight her way through this world as a big butch lesbian. Melissa grew up with two sisters in the Los Angeles-Orange County borderlands of Whittier and La Habra. She's a Fulbright Scholar, writer, and college professor. She also writes about beer and queer culture for the James Beard Award-winning publication, *L.A. Taco*.

CASSANDRA LANE

Cassandra Lane was born and raised in Louisiana in the 1970s. Despite the fact that her great-grandfather was lynched, the earlier generations of her family did not join the Great Migration, that beautiful, dream-filled flock of Black Louisianans who escaped Jim Crow terror for what they hoped would be a safer home in the City of Angels. Lane followed those pioneers' footsteps decades later, settling first in Glendale in 2001. In twenty years, she has lived in seven different apartments and houses across Los Angeles County. Her current South LA neighborhood has remnants of Louisiana all over it—from a New Orleans snoball shop to a jazz and blues club/restaurant called La Louisanne to the crawfish boudin she buys at the corner store—and so feels like home more than any other place she has lived in the City of Angels. Learn more at cassandralane.net.

KENJI C. LIU

From New Jersey, the Lenape homeland, to Los Angeles in the Tongva nation where he now lives, Kenji C. Liu tries to see places through their multiple layers. Little Tokyo is full of them due to colonization, forced eviction, development, redevelopment, and always—resistance and joy. The ecological layer is one he has begun to examine more lately. He spends a lot of time walking and looking at plants and animals everywhere, thinking about how we interact with them in our neighborhoods. It helps him feel connected, and inspires creativity. Find him at kenjiliu.com

ANNABELLE LONG

Annabelle Long is from Sacramento, which, depending on who you ask, is either the City of Trees or America's Farm-to-Fork Capital. She graduated from UC Berkeley, where she walked thousands of miles during the pandemic, wrote a biography of a woman who lived and died in the Midwest, and graduated with highest honors in History. She currently works as a speechwriter and lives in Brooklyn (and misses California every day). You can find more of her writing at annabellelong.com.

SUE MARK

An Oaklander for more than three decades, Sue Mark is a public service artist, cultural researcher, and educator. She co-designs interactive opportunities to amplify and preserve neighborhood narratives at risk of erasure. Standing on the shoulders of the Black Panther Party Survival Programs, Sue founded Commons Archive (2014) to uplift local histories and explore tensions arising from economic and cultural shifts in North Oakland and South Berkeley.

JENISE MILLER

Jenise Miller grew up in the places that once activated the Black Arts Movement in the West. Living in Compton, Long Beach, and Watts, she experienced the beauty of Elliott Pinkney murals and Charles Dickson sculptures. She is the daughter of Panamanian parents and descendant of Black Caribbean Panama Canal workers; migrations, community, and art have shaped her life and her work as a writer and urban planner. Having taken many walks down 103rd Street, she affirms that in the city that never walks, Watts has always been different. Find her work at www.jenisemiller.com.

SAMINA NAJMI

Samina Najmi's writing is a communal story of multigenerational migrations, some prompted by colonial violence in South Asia and others by seductive mythologies of lands that promised new lifeways, if not home. Her students give her definition. Her two children have come to adulthood in Fresno, ancestral home of the Yokuts and Mono peoples, and pulsing heart of the San Joaquin Valley. Samina wrote this essay when she and her then-adolescent children first moved into their Calimyrna Avenue home. And she writes now knowing what it is to long to return to it, after the fire that has redefined home for her once again.

RUTH NOLAN

Ruth Nolan was born in San Bernardino and has lived since childhood in and near the Mojave Desert to work as a wildland firefighter for the Bureau of Land Management's California Desert District and the U.S. Forest Service. She considers every corner of the Mojave Desert home in the deepest, storied sense: from its friendly Joshua tree forests twinkling along its southernmost boundaries all the way north to the raw but life-giving beauty of Death Valley (Timbisha) and east to the Colorado Plateau. The single mother of one daughter and four young grandchildren, she teaches English and creative writing classes at College of the Desert and California Indian Nations College in the Coachella Valley.

DANIEL LANZA RIVERS

Born in Silicon Valley a few years before the '90s tech boom, Daniel Lanza Rivers grew up between Sunnyvale, San Diego, and the East Bay suburbs. Though Daniel spent their childhood summers (and much of grad school) driving "the Five," they mostly stick to I-680 these days—commuting between their home in El Sobrante and their office at San José State. In recent years, Daniel has developed a new appreciation for the 99 freeway, which connects them and their partner, Rowan, to family in Modesto, Escalon, and Oakdale (the "cowboy capital of the world").

BRYNN SAITO

Fourth generation Californian and fourth generation Korean American and Japanese American, Brynn Saito lives in the traditional lands of the Yokuts and Mono peoples, also known as Fresno, California. When she left the Central Valley—as an angsty, art-obsessed eighteen-year-old in search of bigger, brighter cities—she never thought she'd return. But this place—with its grapevine sunsets and perennial dust—called her home. Twenty years later, Brynn has returned to the city of her childhood, where stories of family loss, struggle, and joy awaited.

GEORGE B. SÁNCHEZ-TELLO

George B. Sánchez-Tello drove past his current home every weekend as a child when his family made a regular trek from their house in unincorporated Arcadia in the San Gabriel Valley to El Tepeyac, the iconic Chicano restaurant on Evergreen in Boyle Heights. The Tello-Castillo family arrived in Boyle Heights from Guatemala at the onset of the war, and the Sánchez-Pino-Baca family a generation earlier from their ancestral homelands in New Mexico. He's done investigative reporting in San Francisco, written about punk rock in Salas, Son Jarocho in Tucson, and done Chicano writing in Los Angeles, but George is mostly a father to Quetzal and T'Zu'Nuum and tends to the family garden.

DAVID L. ULIN

David L. Ulin was born and raised in New York, where he learned to think of cities—and to engage with them—through the vehicle of walking, which is also how he has experienced Los Angeles since arriving here in 1991. He wouldn't go so far as to say this is a walking city—but it can be, if you think about it right. He is interested in that tension, between the city of sprawl and the city of neighborhoods, the amorphous and the concrete. Only when we make the city small can we hope to see it, which is what he aspires to do each time he walks its streets.

MARCO VERA

Marco Vera is a *fronterizo* Angeleno who struggles with borders of the mind and soul. If one were to forsake heavy drinking for music, then you'd probably fail at both.

NOTES

CHAPTER 10: IN THE RUBBLE: PICTURING LA'S HOUSING CRISIS

[1] Bill Chandler, "Operation Knockdown news conference Thursday, February 15, 1990—11:00 a.m.," February 14, 1990, Box 3922, Folder 4, Mayor Tom Bradley Administration Papers, Charles E. Young Research Library, University of California Los Angeles.

[2] Warren V. O'Brien and Michael Tharpe, Memo to Mayor Tom Bradley, February 8, 1990, Box 3922, Folder 4, Mayor Tom Bradley Administration Papers, Charles E. Young Research Library, University of California Los Angeles.

[3] Chandler, "Operation Knockdown."

[4] Jill Stewart, "Home Knockdowns Roust More Than Drug Dealers," Los Angeles Times, January 23, 1990, A1.

[5] O'Brien and Tharpe, Memo to Bradley.

CHAPTER 11: CORNTASSEL

Parts of this essay previously appeared in *Echolocation: Songs, Stories and Poems from Indian Country: L.A.* by Carolyn M. Dunn, published by Fezziwig Books in 2013. Copyright is owned by the author.

Writing the Golden State: The New Literary Terrain of California
Edited by Carribean Fragoza, Romeo Guzmán, and Samine Joudat

Illustrations by Fernando Corona

Design by Stephanie Mullins, Steph Says Hello LLC | stephsayshello.com

10 9 8 7 6 5 4 3 2 1

ISBN-13978-1-62640-121-1

Library of Congress Cataloging-in-Publication Data is available

Published by Angel City Press at Los Angeles Public Library
angelcitypress.com

Printed in Canada